HER MOTHER'S BETRAYAL

A journey from horror to happiness

WENDY RICHARDS

ISBN: 978-0-620-83371-4
Printed in the Republic of South Africa by Novus Print

For Ty.
You have helped me become the mother I always wished I had.
You have taught me the true meaning of love.
For the boy you were, and the man you have become, I am forever grateful.
Dream big! Make it happen! I am so proud of you.
I will love you always.
Mum xx

PROLOGUE: GHOSTS AND SHADOWS

I was alone in the dark again.

Looking back on that unrelenting, penetrating blackness, it's hard to imagine how we could possibly hope to combat it with the handful of light bulbs that were scattered throughout the nearly derelict gatehouse my father and I called home. What scant, cold comfort those little glowing curls of tungsten actually offered in the midst of this deep country dark, but how I wished I could have that comfort now.

Dad had left that morning. I had no idea where he was off to. He had various bits of business that took him away from time to time. I didn't mind mostly; I always got on as best I could and I had no complaints about being left to my own devices. If anything, it made me feel mature, accomplished and independent – more like the person I dreamed I would one day become.

Dad and I lived in a rundown lodge in the middle of rural Wales. Buying and renovating old places like this one was something of a hobby of his. He had already done a lot of work on the place by the time I got there – I shuddered to think what it must have looked like before.

To most city dwellers ours would have seemed an idyllic lifestyle – the peace and quiet, "the green and pleasant land." I suppose it was like that, for the most part – certainly compared to the rough English council estate I had lived on before. Nevertheless, on those nights when I was on my own in this abandoned place, and the shadows surrounded me as far as I could see in any direction, there wasn't much to be appreciated in it.

There was no council-supplied electricity here. The building was connected to a noisy, petrol-stinking generator, which seemed to have a mind of its own and worked when it felt like it. Once again, it had decided to take the night off. The dark enveloped and pressed against my teenage mind and body like an unwelcome embrace – a feeling I knew too well.

Not that I was afraid of the dark – there were worse things than that to fear. Here alone though, in literally the middle of nowhere, the unchecked night filled up with unpleasant possibilities, thrown up by my mind in the absence of the dulling, comforting stimulation offered by television. I would have preferred to get into bed and stay there until the sweet relief of morning came but that was not an option: the horses had to be fed.

I grabbed my coat and torch, put on my boots and opened the front door. The damp, bitterly cold air rushed in to greet me as I stepped into the profound darkness of the archway that passed through the gatehouse. I switched on my torch and followed its weak beam, doing my best not to think about the shadows that gathered outside of its narrow scope.

As I walked out from under the arch onto the path that led to the stables, the main lodge house came into view. It stood in stark relief against the night sky, lampless and deserted. I didn't usually like to look up there, especially at night. I always fancied I could see white, wispy shapes flitting around behind the broken panes, staring back at me, lying in wait for my attention, for the lone purpose of frightening me. Something seemed to move there now, in response to my gaze. I looked away quickly. Of course, there was nothing and nobody there. I was alone, completely alone, with not a human soul – living or dead – around for several miles in all directions. That was both a scary and a comforting thought.

If the dark was oppressive, the silence was almost more so. The loud, rhythmic crunching of my boots on the gravel was actually comforting. What troubled me more than either the murk or the silence were the endless nasty possibilities my mind created. The night seemed to come alive with sound – wind through the trees and various animal sounds, not all of which I could identify.

As I walked, the night in front of me became a blank space into which I could project the pictures in my head. A rapid succession of images flashed there now, mostly faces, opaque and indistinct but easily identifiable: my mother's – never really the face of a mother, not then or ever, but that of the stranger she would always be to me. Twisted, filled with a hatred that no mere stranger would feel; my father's face, bland and cheerful, harmless enough in his way; my brother's, wide-eyed, innocent, good-natured – even now the thought of him sent a pang of worry through my stomach.

Among them, other faces appeared and receded quickly – teachers, friends, my foster mother, police officers, care workers. Most distinct and persistent of them all, most intrusive, was his face – imperious, gloating and knowing.

It was mostly that face that haunted me in this darkness. In one way or another, it haunts me still, standing up to long and often tortuous efforts at exorcism.

I stopped for a moment and closed my eyes, shutting it all out. The blackness intensified briefly. Then, another image slowly took shape before me: I was standing on a beach, cool seawater washing over my feet as I looked up at a brilliant blue sky, the sun at the fringe of my vision, pouring warmth and light. Around me, white beach sand extended to the left and right. In front of me, the sand gave way to waves of gorgeous azure. Palm trees swayed in the breeze. I didn't know where this paradise was – probably only in my mind – but I had long since vowed to myself that I would live there one day and I had visualised it so often that it had become habitual. It was no idle daydream – it was my vision, my goal, and I knew, with a certainty I could not quite explain, that it would materialise one day, bringing with it everything I hoped for.

As I stood there, in the cold murk of the Welsh night, my other senses were co-opted into the vision my inner eye was projecting. I could actually feel the sun on my skin, the sand between my toes, the gentle waves rising around my legs. I could smell the seawater and hear the waves crashing. In that moment, for just a while, the gloom and cold of that tumbledown lodge in Wales disappeared, and the ghosts vanished with it.

*

About fifteen years later, I sat in the front seat of a paratrike, a machine similar to a microlight, about to take off into the cool dawn air over the Valley of a Thousand Hills in South Africa's KwaZulu-Natal Province. I was a long way from where I was born and raised, from my best friends and from my family, but I was home – perhaps for the first time in my life. Behind me, in the pilot's seat, was the first man who ever really loved me. He was certainly the first one who treated me like he loved me, and showed none of the behaviours that, for years, I had been brainwashed to think of as love.

We were about to glide westward towards the Drakensberg mountains as the winter sun rose behind us. As the machine took to the air, I was amazed at how smooth its motion was. I looked back over my shoulder and commented on it, shouting over the din of the propeller and wind. He looked at me and laughed, sharing in my exhilaration. For me this was still a novelty but for him, it was what he did every day, a passion that he had successfully turned into a vocation. I was in awe of the beauty I saw unfolding beneath us – mountains, rivers, valleys, miniature towns. Out of the corner of my eye, I saw our shadow coursing along the ground alongside and hundreds of feet below us.

I was reminded of a recurring dream I used to have when I was very young – years before I found myself in among the ghosts and shadows. I had almost forgotten that dream. It came back to me in this moment of fulfilment.

There I was, a successful businesswoman and a mother to a son I loved abundantly, from the core of my soul. My shadow was far removed from me; the sun rising behind me as this wonderful man flew me over a warm and beautiful country I had once only imagined. The ghosts seemed long gone.

"My God," I thought to myself. "How did I get here?"

*

But still they come, from time to time, when I least expect them. They often appear in shapes I don't recognise at first, seeming to hide in unrelated people and experiences. They are in disguise, but they demand my recognition. Sometimes I see them for what they are and, once confronted, they dissipate just as quickly as they materialised. Sometimes I don't recognise them and they wreak havoc in my mind.

Always, though, I have the power to rise above those ephemeral shadows, to watch them pass as my focus rests on the beautiful life my dreams have created. It's a power I have always had, although I didn't always know it, even when I first started using it. It is thanks to this ability that the lonely, broken teenage girl walking in the impenetrable dark in the grounds of a ramshackle Welsh lodge, became the grown woman – successful, loved and in love – flying over the hills of KwaZulu-Natal in the gorgeous early morning sunshine.

*

Back and further back we go, in search of the experiences that made us, hunting for meanings in the memories. For some of them, the only meaning is the sheer bliss of being – like that morning flight, or the moment I held my son in my arms for the first time. Others make no apparent sense at all and I have to dig deep into them: the 'present' I received for my tenth birthday, the days I wanted nothing more than to give up on my dreams and die. So much pain, so many tears, so much blood, so much cold indifference, so much dirt and so many rugs to sweep it under. Those meaningless moments are the ghosts and shadows that have hovered over my life. Today I embrace them – I know that pain is never meaningless. Discovering their meanings, I lay them to rest.

There are any number of moments that could begin this story, regardless of the order in which they have unfolded: a night in Wales, a day in South Africa, an afternoon somewhere in between. That torch-lit trudge to the stables is by no means the start. Neither are most of the other possibilities that come to my mind. Somehow, regardless of how many other scenes I have lived through, endured or enjoyed, it starts here: a little girl lying on her bed, her father standing naked beside her and her mother's blood running down the wall.

CHAPTER ONE: TRELECH

"Just kill me!"

This came out in breathless shrieks, punctuated by the dull, sickening thuds of bone against brick. My mother, her face pulled out of shape in my father's grasp, spat the words out through a grimace of pain. From where I lay on my bed, the two people who had brought me into the world, and who were tasked with guiding me through it, loomed above me. My mother flopped, ragdoll-like, backwards against the wall, held up by Dad's grip on her head, her body lolling weakly back as he repeatedly thrust her head into the wall.

Dad, naked, as he usually was at times like this, stood over both of us, face distorted with rage. None of this was particularly unusual. Moments like these had come and gone in the eight years of my life without having left much of a trace of themselves before the next one came around.

However, this one did leave a trace. Drops of blood now started to appear on the wall behind my mother's head. They multiplied and ran together down over the wooden slats that clad the wall above my bed.

"Go on. Just kill me!" she screamed again.

"You're not worth it," he shouted.

He gave her one last push, then turned and stormed out. She collapsed, putting her hands out to stop herself from falling onto me. I looked up at her but she was not seeing me. Her hand went gingerly to the side of her head and she winced as she touched the area that had just been battered. The blood was caked in her short curls and running down over her ear.

She raised her head and looked at me, snapping out of her inner world of pain, seeing me as if she had not been aware that I was there until that instant. There was only resentment in that gaze, as if somehow, I was to blame, like I had put him up to it. Somewhere in the dark recesses of my young mind, I must have wondered whether there was truth in her silent accusation.

I met her hard, tear-stained gaze. Was she waiting for me to say something? What could I say? She stood and left the room.

"I might as well finish what you started now!" she screamed, her voice fading as she walked down the corridor.

"Go on then. Do us all a favour!" my father's voice snapped back from somewhere else in the house.

That was more or less how it had always happened, for as long as

I could remember. I lay on the bed, my only companion being my teddy bear Bruno, and gazed out of the window. I simply wasn't there anymore. That day, for the first time, I went away to my place in the sun far, far away. I couldn't stop or change what was happening. The best I could do was take myself away from it. So that's what I did. Escaping into a world of imagination is hardly unusual for children but this was different. Over the years, this particular image would gain clarity and focus each time I brought it to mind. I knew that day, just as I would six years later as I stood in the dark with the ghosts, and on many other occasions of far greater stress, that one day I was going to that place – or somewhere better – and there I'd be free and safe. Where exactly the image came from, I don't know. What I was imagining was far outside the world into which I had been born and with which I was familiar. In my head, the sun shone brightly and I was alone, away from all of this. It was somewhere I could be truly happy. My imagination stretched to know what that might feel like.

But in the village of Trelech it was raining... It always rained in Trelech.

*

What a happy family!

A father and husband, smiling and easy going – a horse-owner and saddler, a craftsman and a family man. A mother and wife – gracious, a model of social propriety. Pillars of this rural, horsey Welsh community. They're not rich like some of their peers but they can carry it off at the horse shows they attend on a regular basis. Here is their daughter – at eight, already a seasoned equestrian, parading with ease on the backs of prize show ponies. And there is their four-year-old son, suitably adorable with blonde ringlets and rosy cheeks.

A perfect family.

That was the Steinke family among the horse-and-hound society of South-West Wales. It was by no means an unpleasant environment in which to grow up. It was everything most English people think of when they think of Wales: a tiny village amid breathtaking countryside – horses, foxes and hounds, daffodils and leeks, rural living and parochial mind sets. Although Trelech was only about 200 miles from London, where both my parents had been born and raised, Trelech was really worlds away from that city. What had prompted Robert and Shirley Steinke to make the trek – both physical and cultural – to the edge of civilisation, was my father's profession in, and passion for, the equestrian world. My mother had simply tagged along I suppose. It certainly wasn't her passion; I couldn't actually say whether my mother ever had any passions.

Horses and everything about them were a part of my life from the time I was born. I picked up Dad's interest in the animals and the sport and he was very happy to encourage my inclinations. I think I must have been riding ponies before I could walk. So by the time I was eight, I knew my way around a stable and I was at home in a saddle. My life revolved around horse shows and when I wasn't at one or preparing for one, I would pretend I was.

We lived on a smallholding just outside of the main village, four of the barely 600 souls that called the little hamlet home. Our place was one of Dad's "fixer-uppers" – a farmhouse that was barely liveable when we first arrived. We lived outside the main house in a caravan for what felt like forever. It was, however, quite a large piece of land for a family of fairly humble means, as we were. Aside from horses, we also had a few chickens – and sheep of course, because, after all, what is a Welsh field without sheep!

That was my entire world for the first nine years of my life. Our smallholding and the surrounding fields provided endless space for wandering and exploration. Well, not endless exactly but those acres may as well have been an entire universe as far as I was concerned. I set out one rare sunny day on those rolling greens – I can't remember how old I was exactly. I wasn't looking for anything in particular. It was just that the aimless liberty of the fields was far more appealing than the cramped quarters of the caravan where I had only my mother's ill-disguised misery for company.

Only a few yards from the house, the fields opened up into untamed grazing land. With the house out of sight and our nearest neighbour far over on the other side, it was easy for me to pretend that I was the only person in the world. There was a deep inner security in that aloneness, as I veered off the well-trodden path into the grass. With the familiar scent of fresh animal droppings in my nostrils, I walked in the general direction of a flock of grazing sheep as they made their way slowly from one grazing patch to another. I was looking down at my feet as I walked, so I couldn't miss what now came into sight just ahead of the toe of my right shoe: partly covered in dirty white fleece, partly pink and fleshy. I bent to pick it up and examined it, holding it between my thumb and forefinger. It obviously hadn't been here long. It probably had only just dropped off one of the lambs that were now cavorting in the care of their elders. I knew about the practice – Dad had told me about it – but I had never actually seen it happen. Farmers would place docking rings around newborn lamb's tails, to cut off circulation so the tail would eventually drop off. It was just another of the procedures that went with farm life. I took that tiny piece of discarded flesh and bone and put it in my pocket.

From that day on, whenever I had a chance, I would hunt those fields high and low for those little remnants. I can't remember what I did with them but I felt compelled to collect them. It seemed a shame to just let them lie where they had fallen, those morsels of innocence, withered and shed as a first lesson to their owners of the realities of life. Not that I thought in those terms at such a young age, of course. Looking back, though, could I see some commonalities between myself and those lambs? Was I somehow trying to recover something that seemed irreparably lost?

*

For a long time before I turned ten, I used to have a recurring dream. I would find myself flying high above a lush, sunbathed green forest, stretching as far as my eyes could see. I was 'swimming' through the air in a kind of breaststroke movement, absolutely weightless, the wind rushing through my hair, in control of everything – my speed, my direction, my altitude. The feeling was intense and palpable: the sense of lightness, the sheer joy of unconstrained movement, the total absence of fear. I would have this vivid dream almost every night. Yet, by the time I took that real flight over the Drakensberg Mountains years later, I had almost completely forgotten about it. It was only then that the dream came back to me. In the dream I was alone but never lonely. From a very young age, I knew the difference between those two states. I also understood that I could feel both even when I was surrounded by people. Whether I was wandering the fields around Trelech on my own, or at home, navigating my way through the congealed mutual hatred that hung in the air between my parents, I was alone either way. But in the confines of home, in the bosom of my family, I felt real loneliness, and only the sweet, genuine solitude of the fields and hills could relieve it.

So, by the time I was nine, I was most comfortable in my own company. I knew how to drive myself, how to entertain myself, how to dream dreams and set goals for myself. Considering what was to come, there was no better lesson that Trelech could have taught me.

*

My little bright yellow, AA-branded go-cart was the closest thing I had to a fulfilment of my flying dreams. I would take it to the top of our slightly inclined quarter-mile driveway and then let it ride all the way down, building up speed as I went, letting gravity pull me forward. My little black and white mixed-breed dog Lucy ran along beside me, barking happily. When I wasn't riding a pony, I was riding that cart. It never took me as far as I would have liked of course, but the sheer joy of motion brought its own reward.

My little Lucy was my only steadfast companion through those years. Whatever I was doing, she was usually trotting along beside me. I can't remember exactly how many litters of puppies she had in her life. Nobody ever thought to get her spayed. I remember several adorable little balls of fluff brought into the world by Lucy and removed from it by the hard necessities of life. A few weeks after one litter had been born, I noticed Dad carrying a bucket of water. There was nothing remarkable about that. We had no running water so whenever we needed it, it came by the bucketful, which Mum would usually fetch from the river. What was unusual was what happened next. My dad gathered up the pups from where they were nestling with their mother and proceeded to hold them under the water, one by one, until their tiny lives were extinguished. Nothing malicious or anything – just the way life went apparently – too many mouths to feed.

I had witnessed Dad beating my mother on a semi-regular basis for as long as I could remember. It had reached the point of routine and it seldom prompted much more of a reaction from me than avoidance – the desire to keep quiet and out of the way. If I had ever felt any sense of injustice over it, it had long since been numbed. This was too much though. The sight of those adorable, innocent little creatures simply being disposed of – it made me sick and sad to my core.

However, dad was an adult. He knew better. There was nothing to be said. I turned and walked away, only to be met by my mother standing at the backdoor of the house.

"This is how life is," she said, regarding me with an unmovable, glassy stare. "The sooner you get used to it, the better off you'll be."

I ran then, into the fields, down to the bottom of the property, where the stream marked the boundary of our world. I sat alongside it for I don't know how long, watching the water flow freely away, never to return. One day I would be just like those rapids and ripples. Like them, I was only passing through this place and I wouldn't stop here longer than I needed to before heading on my way to bigger and better things.

Some days later, I came back to the stream with a bottle, inside of which was a note I had written to whomever may find it. I can't remember what I wrote. I don't know whether it was a cry for help or just some trivial message about whatever was occupying my mind at the time. Either way it was my first attempt to reach out to a world beyond this one, a world where love and friendship, fun and excitement waited. It was the first of many messages in bottles that I sent out in that stream. I hoped that it would be carried over the rocks into the River Teifi, and away into the sea beyond, to be found and read by someone far, far away, who may one day come and find me. Maybe it would smash against a rock and sink, but maybe it would drift out into the Irish Sea and the Atlantic Ocean beyond, washing up on a beach in Jamaica or the Bahamas. Maybe someone would read the letter, wonder who Wendy Steinke was and want to know more about me. Maybe my long-lost real parents would discover it and come and find me. I wished that might happen, because I certainly didn't feel like I belonged to the parents I had. There was hope in the mere fact that those bottles were going anywhere at all. If they could be carried off to lands far away from here, then so could I, and my time would come.

As it turned out, I wasn't to spend too much longer in the village of Trelech. The old farmhouse and the acres on which it stood would soon be a part of my history.

Trelech – that lonely piece of south Wales, which doesn't even appear on any but the most detailed of maps, was my world for nine years. Home of sheep and dogs and horses and streams and go-carts. That cold little corner of nowhere, but home nonetheless, for a while. While I was there, I took it for granted, as children do. There were times when I even scorned it as I wished to be elsewhere.

But before long, I would miss it.

CHAPTER TWO: UNEXPECTED GIFTS

"There are moments in life that define us. Even more than the events them-selves, how we process and respond to them will define who we are for the rest of our lives, imprinting on our souls forever."

A few months after my ninth birthday, my parents gave me the best present I could ever have asked them for: they sat me down and announced to me that I was adopted. It didn't come as a shock; deep down I had always known I wasn't theirs. We were alien to each other, we all knew it. Finally the cat was out of the bag. There was no real emotion when they told me; my mother was as cold as always and Dad was his usual upbeat self.

"We never intended to tell you," Dad said as he raised his coffee mug to his lips. "But we got a call the other day…" He watched me for a moment over the rim of his cup. "It's your real mum. Her situation has changed and she's decided she wants to meet you and see if perhaps you want to go and live with her."

I turned my gaze away from Dad to my mother. She had been looking down at the floor and now met my gaze briefly, a faint smile crossing her face. Happy to be rid of me. The feeling was mutual.

"Who is she?" I asked.

"Not sure," Dad replied. "A bit of a toff, by the sound of things. She's away on an overseas trip at the moment. Apparently she's always jetting off somewhere or other. She wants to meet you when she gets back."

I felt dizzy, but in a good way. Reality had been pulled out from under me – and I couldn't have been more thrilled. Instead of falling, I was floating. My real mother, a cultured and well-to-do jetsetter was coming to get me. She would gather me up in her arms and tell me how she never meant to give me up, and how sorry she was. Then she would take me home and she would let me go with her on her trips around the world. Maybe she would finally take me to my place in the sun. I thought I was dreaming.

*

Dreaming was exactly what I was doing.

That was just one of the scenarios I concocted while gazing out of the window on rainy days or walking through the fields. Around my ninth birthday, these fantasies became more frequent: a hundred different ways in which I would discover that I was not a Steinke at all. Shortly after I had reached that milestone, something happened that gave me a sudden surge of hope that it may actually happen.

Dad and Mum were having a row again. I didn't know what it was about. It didn't really matter – they would always find something to fight over. But this time was different. This time it didn't end with blows and blood and screams, followed by that thick, uncomfortable silence. I was sitting in the lounge, my back turned to the front window, when Dad stormed past me with a suitcase in his hand. He slammed the front door behind him and I turned to watch him go. Behind me, my mother emerged from the kitchen, shouting. I can't remember what she was saying. When Dad heard her, he suddenly stopped and put down his suitcase. He bent, picked up a brick and lobbed it towards the window with all his strength. It crashed through the glass. Luckily I was low enough so that the brick came nowhere near me, flying directly over me towards my mother. I was right next to the window, however, and the large pane dissolved into a cascade of tiny shards that showered over my head. Had he even seen me there? Did he even care?

That was how I found out my parents were getting divorced.

In the days that followed, I nurtured a flicker of hope that now that they were splitting up, the adoption talk would finally come, but of course it didn't. All I found out was that Dad had met another woman – a seventeen-year-old named Lisa – and he was going to live with her. My brother and I would have to stay with our mother and we wouldn't be able to live on our free holding in Trelech anymore.

I don't know how I felt about the divorce. It wasn't as if things had been great while they were together, so there was actually some hope that the separation might make life better.

*

"I think it's time you saw this." My mother was standing outside the caravan that served as Dad's workshop. No doubt he would be taking it away before long. She opened the door and went in and I followed close behind, wondering what she could possibly want to show me. She took me through the workshop, with its lingering warm smell of leather. Whatever it was that I was supposed to see was not here in the main working area. My mother went to a small room at the back of the caravan and pulled open the door.

"There," she said. "Come and see what your father's really like."

I peered in and saw nothing but magazines. Scores of them, neatly stacked on shelves and the floor. My mother picked one up, opened it at random and showed it to me. I didn't really understand why the woman staring up from the page was naked or what her hooded-eyed, open-mouthed stare was supposed to portend but there was an instinctive sense that this was something somehow forbidden, dirty. I couldn't help but snigger nervously.

"Why would Dad want books full of naked ladies, Mum?"

"This is what men are. This is how they see us, this is all we are to them and your father's no different." There was a moment of the briefest hesitation, a softening in her usually stony bearing. She placed her hand on one of the stacks of magazines and glanced away from me for a second, as if rethinking her decision to bring me here. But the frost was back in her eyes when she turned to look at me again. "I don't think you can ever be too young to learn this. I wish my mother had told me when I was your age. She might have saved me a lot of trouble."

I still wasn't quite following. I was completely innocent to sex – it had not so much as blipped on my radar, not even in the furtive, ill-informed whispers of schoolmates.

"Why does he need so many?" I asked. "How many naked ladies does he want to look at?"

"One's never enough for any of them," she answered with a hard, humourless smile. "It's a pity we can't do without them entirely."

"The magazines?" I was properly confused now.

"No, men."

*

Considering my mother's distaste for men, I was surprised at how quickly she got another one in her life after Dad left. It was only a matter of months before she started seeing Stephen. He was apparently a former resident of Trelech who had come back to town and had been introduced to both my parents by mutual friends. Being only nine years old at the time, I have no idea how Steve's courtship of my mother began but it must have all happened rather quickly. All I knew was that, before long, he was a regular and then constant presence in our lives.

I never quite knew what to make of him. From the first day, I noted his signature smell: a blend of stale sweat and the milky instant coffee he drank all the time. He had beady, black eyes that always seemed haughty and calculating. But it was nice to have him around because he took the edge off being around my mother, countering her harsh energy with kind words, laughter and a willingness to offer presents or suggest fun activities for me and my brother to do.

His arrival coincided with the approach of my tenth birthday. There was something exciting about heading for that first double digit. To my mind, I was about to become a 'big girl'. My parents had never made much of a fuss about birthdays and I had no reason to expect either of them to do anything to celebrate.

A week or so before my birthday, Steve came into my room as I was getting ready for bed.

"Come on then," he said. "In you get."

I got into bed and he pulled the covers up over me. He sat on the edge of the bed and looked at me, as if studying me, a mysterious smile on his face.

"I hear you've got a birthday coming up," he said after a second.

I smiled and nodded.

"And how old are you turning?"

"Ten," I replied eagerly.

"Wow. So you're becoming a big girl then?"

My smile expanded.

"A big girl needs a big birthday present," he said, putting his hand to his chin as if contemplating. "How would you like to take a little trip with me to celebrate your birthday?"

"Where to?" I asked, immediately excited at the prospect.

"Well we can go to my place and stay there a few days."

I beamed at him.

"And when we get there, you'll get a present befitting a big girl.

Something really special. What do you say?"

I think my bright eyes and big smile must have given him the answer he was looking for.

"Good, it's settled then."

He stood up and turned off the light, pausing at the door for just a moment. "Good night, birthday girl."

"Good night," I answered as my mind swam with all the possibilities this birthday could bring. I lay in the dark before sleep came, imagining the trip. Considering the divorce and everything that went with it, I certainly didn't expect my parents to do much this year for my birthday, no matter how big the milestone. But now there was a celebration just for me – a celebration of me. Well, I thought, maybe I could really get to like smelly old Steve. With images of open roads and yet-to-be-explored cities floating through my head – not to mention wild imaginings of what that big present could be – please let it be a Barbie doll – I finally drifted off to sleep.

*

A couple of weeks later, the day came and Mum helped me pack a bag, which Steve then loaded into his car. I was surprised to learn that Mum and my brother weren't going to come with us – it would just be Steve and me. "This is your holiday, Wendy," Steve told me. "We'll do something fun with them when we get back."

Before I got into the car, Mum came and said goodbye, saying repetitively: "Be a good girl." She also said a couple of other things before that but I wasn't really listening. She was being serious and I wasn't in the mood for that – this was my birthday. Of course I would be a good girl – I always was.

As fields, roads and towns stretched and passed around, before and behind us, I kept my face glued to the passenger side window, taking it all in. The world was finally revealing itself to me. My thoughts again went to the present that was waiting for me. All my toys up to that point had leaned towards the "boyish": my go-cart, farmyard playsets and so on. I had decided it was time to be a bit more girlish as I went into my tenth year. So many girls at school had Barbie dolls and I hoped I was also getting one at last. But then again, I thought to myself, it might be something even better. My mind freely explored the possibilities as we drove along.

I'm not sure how far into the four-hour trip we were when Steve interrupted my passenger window daydreams by putting his hand on my leg. We had made idle chitchat before but then, as we progressed, the car settled into silence as often happens on long journeys. I turned to look at him.

"There's a really big present for you when we get there," he said. "A big present for a big girl." Then he moved his hand up my inner thigh, under my dress, until he could reach between my legs. He started to stroke me through my underwear and I tensed up. I didn't know what he was doing or what it meant, but I knew that he wasn't supposed to. I knew I didn't like it. He must have felt my tension because he took his hand away, gave me a reassuring smile, and then turned his eyes back to the road. The trip continued in silence.

As we headed east, the roads became busier and the towns became bigger – villages and isolated farmhouses giving way to suburbs, which, in turn, were replaced by dense council estates and tower blocks. After what felt like forever, we drove into the parking area of one of those barely distinguishable grey giants.

Steve switched off the car and turned to me with a smile.

"Here we are, big girl. Are you ready for your present?"

I nodded, which made him smile all the more.

We made our way upstairs to his flat, our feet echoing on the cement stairs and floors. The heavy, hollow clack of his shoes and the softer, quicker patter of my trainers, totally out of time with each other, their sounds mingling with the unfamiliar noise of nearby traffic. We passed what seemed like a thousand heavy wooden doors, each alike and finally stopped at one just like all the others. He put his key in the lock and pushed the door open, then led the way inside, carrying our bags. I followed and saw his tiny one-bedroomed flat for the first time. It had been standing empty for some time and as I walked in, the stale air assaulted my nostrils. He didn't seem to smell it. If he did, he didn't seem to mind.

Innocent though I might have been, I now started to feel the faintest sense of unease. The door swung closed. It didn't slam, it wasn't loud, but it closed solidly, firmly and with undeniable finality – like a prison door closing behind an inmate.

I will never forget that sound.

"Come on," Steve said, taking our bags and heading down the small passage towards the bedroom. "I'll show you where you're sleeping." I followed him through to the room. Despite my rising misgivings, I was still excited about the possibilities of my birthday celebrations. Besides, I had no reason to mistrust Steve. He was an adult – adults were all to be trusted. Mum and Dad, my teachers. They all knew better than I did. If I couldn't trust them, who could I trust?

Steve walked into the room and put the bags down. I came in behind him and he turned to look at me, tilting his head to one side and studying me closely.

"You're so pretty," he said.

Then he closed the bedroom door behind me. Its heavy, dry click was every bit as forbidding as the front door's. He ran his hand through my hair and brought it to rest under my chin. Then he picked me up and lay me down on the bed. He undressed me and then himself.

"What is this?" I thought to myself. There was no fear as such, just confusion, and a sense of shame, a dirty feeling. We weren't supposed to be nude in front of each other. The sight of his swollen nakedness filled me with embarrassment. Maybe this was something that was supposed to happen when you became a big girl, I thought. Then he got onto the bed with me, his movements, which had been slow and assured before, now more urgent. What was he doing? Why was he getting so close?

Now I was scared. It seemed like he was trying to fall on me, to get closer to me than it was possible to get. The sense of repulsion that now arose in me was like nothing I had ever felt before.

Then the pain came – a sharp, stabbing pain between my legs, seeming to emanate outwards to my extremities. I gasped and held my breath, hoping it would go away quickly. I had never known such pain, or such a sense of utter humiliation.

When he had finished, he stood up, his breathing slowly returning to normal, and pulled on his clothes.

"The bathroom's just to the right if you want to wash up," he said softly – with a strange, inappropriate tenderness. Then, like that, he left the room and I was alone, feeling the repugnant wetness between my thighs.

"What just happened?" I almost said aloud as I stared at the ceiling, hot tears rolling down my cheeks.

From the little kitchen down the passage, I heard the click and hiss of a kettle being put on.

My mother's voice echoed in my head – the words she had said to me quietly but emphatically before I got in the car. "Be a good girl," she had said. But there was something else before that, which I had put out of my mind in my eagerness to get going.

"Steve's going to be taking care of us from now on. So do what he wants you to do. Be a good girl."

There are moments in life that define us. Even more than the events themselves, how we process and respond to them will define who we are for the rest of our lives, imprinting on our souls forever. This was probably my first moment of definition. Barely ten years old, I had just been raped for the first time of many. Nothing could have prepared me for what was to come.

CHAPTER THREE: ON THE EDGE OF
THE ABYSS

I don't know how long I had talked for. I had thought long and hard about what I was going to say but when the moment came, there was no controlling how it would flow. Once the floodgates opened it all tumbled out. Three years is a long time, especially in the life of a child – 1 095 days, 26 280 hours, 1 576 800 minutes, 94 608 000 seconds, ticking by in moments of silent desperation, routine drudgery and wild daydreams of escape.

When I felt like it had all been said, I fell quiet, sitting in my chair in front of the headmaster's desk. He didn't say anything for what felt like forever, although it was probably only a few seconds. The look he gave me was attentive but otherwise unreadable. Whatever emotional responses he may have felt probably tempered by hardened, professional caution. My English teacher sat beside me, her face full of sympathy. She had heard the story before, which is what had led her to bring me here to the headmaster's office. The two of them shared a worried glance.

The headmaster looked back at me then, and spoke with deep concern and extreme kindness. It was a welcome change to get this reaction from adults, in contrast to what I was used to from my mother. I was relieved. Finally I had told it all. It was out and there were people who would help me.

"Wendy," he said, "we have to report this to the authorities. There are people who are specially trained to deal with this kind of situation and we'll have to call them in."

I nodded. He hesitated for a moment, as if carefully considering his next words, then said, "And of course, we'll have to speak to your mother."

I felt a momentary surge of anxiety at that. I couldn't actually predict exactly how she would respond.

"If we call your mother and tell her what you've said, what do you think she'll say?"

I thought for a second. Mum was a hard woman and she often acted like I was a burden to her but she was still my mother.

"She'll support me." Looking back, considering all that had

already happened and was still to come, I'm amazed that I actually believed that.

He nodded and gave me a reassuring smile. I sat back in my chair with a long, heavy exhale. I had done it. At last, I thought, steps would be taken, I would be safe.

*

It's amazing how easily life goes on even when you're trapped in a situation that, by every meaningful standard, should not be born for even a second.

A short while after my tenth birthday, Mum, my brother and I moved in with Steve in his new house in southeast England. I was his now and I could see no way out of that. Was that what he had always wanted? Had he courted my mother just to get to me or had he only noticed me later? Either way, even though, as far as the outside world was concerned, he was my mother's boyfriend, behind closed doors, it was me that held the majority of his interest. He worked during the day, Mum worked at night, which was perfect for him. The daily routine set in pretty quickly. I would come home from school, homework would be done. Steve would come home, supper would be prepared. Then my mother would leave for work, the supper dishes would be cleared away and a board game would usually come out.

I hated it when the board games approached their conclusion. The dread intensified as the pieces on the board moved closer to the end. I would opt for something like Monopoly simply because it could go on for so long. I would try to draw out the game as long as possible, because when the time came to fold up the board and put the dice and counters back in their plastic packets, and my brother was sent to bed, it was very clear what the next event in the evening's proceedings would be.

In those moments when my brother made his way to bed and I sat in terrible anticipation of what was to come, I often remembered an odd thing that happened back in Trelech. We had chickens on the free holding there, together with a large and quite aggressive cockerel. For a long time during the renovations, we hadn't been able to occupy the house and we were living in the caravan outside. At some point, my dad had hung a swing from one of the beams in what would become the lounge. One day, as I was playing outside, I heard my brother screaming in the house. I ran in to find him sitting in the swing, curled up in terror as the cockerel attacked him. I had to run in to rescue him from the crazed bird and had been protective over him ever since. Later, on those nights during that seemingly unending prison sentence in Steve's house, when I felt the urge to resist, I thought of my brother and the possibility that if I did put up a fight, Steve might turn his attentions on him somehow. I couldn't contemplate that possibility. I had to prevent it from happening, even if it meant bearing the brunt of Steve's sickness.

Yes, I was his now – and would be for three years. He had staked his claim long before the move. During that week that he had taken me away for my birthday, he had raped me on a daily basis – often more than once a day. We would go out to walk his dog and he would bring along a blanket so he could have sex with me behind a bush somewhere. When we got back to his flat, he might feel like doing it again. Then when bedtime came, it would happen yet again. He was like some kid enjoying the novelty of a new toy. I think that's all I was to him. Who I was, my thoughts and feelings, the fact that I was a vulnerable child, all meant nothing. I was just a doll for his amusement. Always, he would tell me how pretty I was and how this was all boys would ever want from me.

Before we moved in with him, we lived for a short time with my grandparents, with whom he had done a very good job of ingratiating himself. I remember how he would sit in the lounge, with my grandparents in the kitchen next door, just out of sight, chatting to them as he sat me on his lap and sneaked his hand between my legs. By the time we moved in with him, he had firmly established his ownership of me.

The life of ponies and farmyards and lamb's tails scattered in fields was far behind me now. We lived in a house on a rough council estate near Aldershot, Hampshire – famous as the "home of the British Army".

In and around our council estate, life simply flowed onwards. I went to school every day, I did what I was supposed to do, I was a decent student, and not a single teacher or fellow pupil would ever have imagined what was happening at home. I was a good girl, a normal girl, in a normal family. I had instinctively learned to dissociate two aspects of myself, essentially creating two different parts of me: the stable, in control, affable girl that the rest of the world saw; and the hopeless, unhappy soul that I knew myself to be at heart. I was on the verge of an abyss, at risk of falling in at any moment. It yawned in front of me like a monstrous mouth, ready to swallow me. But for the benefit of the outside world I became very adept at pretending it wasn't there.

There were occasional reprieves from the nightmare when I would go to Wales to visit my dad. At least there, I wasn't subject to Steve's constant attention. At Dad's I could relax and be myself without any fear. The price for that was a nearly complete lack of attentiveness from Dad, but I could manage that – it had never been any other way. There were times when that added to my pain, however. I remember the time when I was left waiting in the car for an hour or more on a midwinter night while my Dad went into Lisa's house for a con-jugal visit. Then there was the time I fell from my pony and injured my hand. Dad wrapped it up and we were soon on our way back to Aldershot. It was only some time after I had arrived back and Dad was already on his way home that we discovered I had broken my wrist. It's strange that the pain hadn't announced the existence of something more serious than a mere sprain hours before. But I think I was so numb that I barely noticed. The pain of a broken bone was nothing compared to the continuous dull ache I felt in my heart all the time.

It never occurred to me that it could get any worse but when I was about 12, it did. In that year, I started having my period – which only added more awkwardness and shame to the entire situation. There was no chance of talking to my mother about it. She was a closed door in every way. The only way I even knew what periods were was because of school. Were it not for that, the arrival of my first one would have taken me completely by surprise. I don't remember even mentioning it to my mother but I must have, because, without any further discussion, she provided the necessary care products. It's funny, looking back, that it never occurred to her that she hadn't taught me about any of this – not so much as the briefest talk. How did she think I had found out about it? Regardless, I took it in my stride, as all girls do, and carried on.

Steve was very interested in this development. He started to use protection and he took an interest in my cycles – a further invasion of my life and an added dimension to the position of sick, uninvited intimacy he held there. Despite the measures he took, something went wrong, because – inevitably – one month, my usual time came and went. Like the fanatical planner and list maker I had been since I was very young, I had a very precise knowledge of my cycle. I had made a point of being knowledgeable about it. When I noted that I was late, I knew immediately what had happened. I felt it, I understood with absolute certainty. Three months passed and it wasn't long before all the signs of early pregnancy started to present themselves. If my mother had any clue, she didn't say so. Steve might have suspected as well – in fact, it was he who took me to the doctor one day. I was mortified when I was asked if I was sexually active. Under Steve's cool gaze, I denied that I was. The doctor didn't press the matter. He could have gone ahead with a pregnancy test but I had told him I wasn't having sex so he ruled it out. That was that.

I can't even remember what I thought or felt about the pregnancy. Perhaps I did feel a certain amount of hopeful doubt that there was some other explanation. Or maybe my despair was already so deep that I saw this as just one more thing to add to my miserable situation. What difference did it make? I was already on the edge of a bottomless pit; I might as well just dive in.

It all came to a head one night in a routine fight between my mother and me. We argued often so there was nothing remarkable about this particular row. The subject of the argument escapes me completely now – probably something trivial. It escalated quickly, though and, in a desperate attempt to make her hear me, I resorted to a tactic I had witnessed her using with my father repeatedly: I threatened to kill myself. She looked at me with a twisted spiteful smile and gave me exactly the response she used to get from Dad: "Well go on then. Do us all a favour. You might as well, because no-one will ever love you anyway."

I don't recall if I was bluffing to begin with, or if I seriously intended to end my life. Either way, I was compelled to escalate the situation, if for no other reason, at least in the hope that someone would care enough to stop me. I went to the bathroom cabinet, took out all the medication I could find, from headache tablets to cough syrup to prescribed antibiotics that had probably long since reached their expiry date, and I began to swallow the lot, with my mother and Steve looking on, making no attempt to intervene, only taunting and prodding me.

It had been my painful and frustrating experience, over the course of the past two years, that nothing ever changed. No matter how desperate I got, things just flowed on as usual. This was an attempt to change that. Something drastic was about to happen: either I would die or they would see how terrible the situation was and put a stop to it. Much to my despair, it didn't go in either of these directions. My mother went to work as normal and I went to bed, still very much alive, hoping that the drugs were simply delayed rather than ineffective. Wondering what the point of anything was, feeling utterly alone and unloved, I simply drifted off to sleep, with the faint prospect that I might never wake up.

I don't know how much later it was that I awoke, my body wracked by terrible cramps and the sheets slick with blood. Steve must have heard my cries because it wasn't long before he burst into my room. He didn't show any emotion, he just discretely and clinically removed the bedding and my bloodied pyjamas, changed both, threw the soiled clothes and linen in the wash, put me back to bed and returned to the room he shared with my mother. Simple as that: no drama or a single word of acknowledgement that I, this twelve-year-old girl, had just miscarried the child he had put in me. No words of comfort – hardly any words at all.

*

Even after all that, still nothing changed. My brother was oblivious to all of it of course, Steve carried on as if nothing had happened and my mother never found out. The following day, although I was dazed and sad at the fact that I hadn't managed to die during the course of the night, I just got up and went to school. The fact that I had been pregnant and just lost a child would not really hit home until decades later.

The abuse did become less frequent but continued nonetheless. In the midst of the ongoing, crushing routine, with my mother ignoring me and Steve continuing to use me however he wanted, I felt like I was constantly on the verge of screaming, like something inside me was about to burst. One day, as my mother was on her way out to work and I had only the prospect of another night alone with Steve to look forward to, my desperation spilled over. In a manic attempt to get my mother's attention and to keep Steve at bay, I actually tried to scratch my eyes out. I dug my fingers into the sockets and tried to pull my eyeballs out. Thankfully, I succeeded only in making my eyes red and swollen. My mother just told me not to be stupid and went on her way. I think it must have scared Steve though; he didn't touch me that night.

The pregnancy and miscarriage were the last straw for me. Although I was in a state of deep depression and constantly being taught that I was unloved and not worth loving, there was a part of me that knew I deserved better and that I owed it to myself to take action. I promised myself that I was going to stop all of it. It had begun on my tenth birthday and I swore that it would end before my thirteenth. But I had no idea how I was going to do it and it took a long time to pluck up the nerve. I would often see TV adverts for Childline and fantasise about making that call. I came so close at times. I would pick up the phone and never dial. On two occasions, I actually did – but I hung up as soon as I heard a voice on the other end of the line. Then, one day, someone answered and I actually stayed on the line. I can't recall the exact details of the exchange but I do remember the simple, lifesaving advice the person gave me – five simple words: "You have to tell someone." As the routine went on, I dreamt and wished about a way out but I just couldn't see it yet. Who could I tell? What would happen if I did? How would Steve react? What about my brother? How would it affect his life if it all came into the open?

Ultimately, it came out unexpectedly when my best friend got it out of me somehow. I can't even remember how. I had been so ready to burst for so long that it only took the slightest prompting from a person I really trusted to bring it all flooding out.

"You have to tell someone," she said. That was all I had been dreaming about for months but now that she actually said it, now that it appeared on the verge of becoming reality, I backtracked.

"Tell who? What am I going to say?"

"One of the teachers. Just tell them what you've told me. You have to. If you don't then I will. I'm giving you till the end of the day."

I think I counted every second as they ticked by that day. I watched the clock as if my life depended on it, putting off the task till the very last minute. I was very fond of my English teacher and I knew that, if I were going to tell any of the school staff, it would be her. How could I approach her with this? Where would I even start? Finally, the bell rang and I knew the moment had come. The classroom seemed to take forever to clear as I dawdled at my desk. My friend looked at me and I gave her a silent signal not to worry – I was going to do it. As the last of my classmates made their way out of the front door, I walked up to the teacher's desk. She looked at me and smiled.

"See you tomorrow, Wendy."

I froze for what appeared to me to be an eternity. She looked at me curiously, expectantly and it took all the strength I had not to just say "Bye then," and run for the door, but I knew there was no turning back. I swallowed my hesitation and took a deep breath.

"I have to tell you something," I murmured softly.

*

It was only an hour or so later that I found myself sitting in the headmaster's office, assuring him and myself that my mother would be on my side. Everything from that point on passed in a strange haze. Two women arrived at the school – the social workers assigned to my case. Their kindness and understanding, combined with an air of authority, made me feel safer than I had felt in my life. It was going to be okay.

The social workers didn't expect me to talk through all the details again. They must have got the gist of the story from the headmaster. They asked me some basic questions and spent most of their time offering what reassurance they could. It was explained to me that we would go to the police and lay a charge against Steve. Of course, my mother, as my legal guardian, would have to lay the charge. So the next step was to call her and get her down to the school.

I sat and waited as they left the room to make the call. What was going through my head in those minutes before my life took that next, decisive turn? I can't really remember – mostly a blend of relief and disbelief that I had finally done it. I didn't have the slightest conception of what would follow. I hadn't really thought that far ahead. All the adults around me had been so caring and helpful and seemingly so in control, so sure in their knowledge of how to handle the situation. Yet all of them exuded an underlying sense of worry and uncertainty. I had no way of knowing that they were surely considering all manner of problems, potential complications and scenarios. Might any of them have questioned my truthfulness? That may have been a consideration for them but it never occurred to me that anyone could think I could make up such a story.

After a few minutes, one of the social workers came back into the office, sat down next to me and looked at me intently.

"Wendy, I just had a talk with your mum," she said.

"Is she coming?"

There was a brief but noticeable pause before her response.

"No, Wendy. She won't be coming."

"What did she say?"

"Wendy, I have to ask you this. Are you absolutely sure that everything you've said is true?"

I felt a stab of indignation. "Yes, of course."

"Do you promise that everything you've said to us is exactly what happened?"

"Yes!"

She studied me closely.

"Okay," she said at last. "I believe you." She averted her eyes, looking anxiously away before continuing. "But, Wendy, your mum…"
I felt a sinking sensation in my stomach, but certainly no real surprise.
"Your mum says she won't come and that we're not to believe what you say. She told us that none of what you've said is true."

I had thought that just telling somebody about my life over the past three years would put an end to my terrible situation. Even now, as I tried to process what the social worker was saying, I didn't realise that this was only the beginning of that process – and it was going to be a long and painful one.

CHAPTER FOUR: ON THE FIRST RUNG

I was in a new home at last. I was safe. I stood at the window of my new bedroom one afternoon, seeing the world from a new perspective. On the street below, cars passed by on their way to wherever they were going, their drivers neither looking in my direction, nor caring that I was looking at them. My foster family were downstairs; they didn't really mind what I was up to, so long as I wasn't dead. My mother was at home, refusing to speak to me, probably happy to have me out of her sight. I was alone… and I was relieved. Being alone meant I was free.

A car I knew all too well suddenly crept into my field of vision, slowing down as it passed the house. He did this almost every day, now that I was out of his house. Of course he knew where I was, it was no secret. It didn't help that my foster home was in the same council estate as his place and located on a street that he had to use to get to and from work every day.

I had set my foot on the first rung of the ladder that would take me out of the personal hell I had lived in for three years, but the climb had only just begun. In the months that followed that moment of revelation in the headmaster's office, I started to wonder if I would ever move to the next step. When I had decided to approach my teacher that afternoon, I actually had no conception of what would happen next. It was just important that I tell somebody. Beyond that, I had trusted that the right people would be called and the necessary steps would be taken. It wasn't going to be quite that easy.

For Social Services, the most important thing had been to get me out of Steve's house and they had done that speedily. From that point on, the wheels turned with grinding slowness. I remember the next few months as a succession of police interviews, followed by a slew of deliberations, discussions and more interviews. Steve denied everything of course and my mother backed him up. She had to, because if he were ever convicted, she would be tried as an accomplice. To this day, I still don't know if she took his side just to save her own skin, or because she genuinely didn't believe me, or because she knew what was going on and didn't care. Whatever the case might have been, I was out of their hands now – but unfortunately we were neighbours.

One day, I was walking home from school with a friend when a nagging instinct prompted me to turn and look towards the road. There he was, driving along slowly behind us. There was a brief moment of eye contact between us and then he sped up and drove off. I turned around and ran back to the school. My foster mother had to come and fetch me.

Not only did my mother refuse to cooperate with the authorities, she also threw wild accusations in my direction. To hear her tell it, not only was I a liar, I was also the neighbourhood prostitute. Either she or Steve even went so far as to plant condoms and cash in a jacket of mine as "proof". I wondered then, and have thought many times since, if indeed I had been a prostitute at the age of twelve, what would that have said about her? What kind of mother would that have made her? She didn't seem to care that, in the act of trying to shift responsibility away from her and her boyfriend, she was still managing to cast herself in a terrible light.

Steve was not supposed to come anywhere near the police station and Social Services office when I was there, but he would often talk his way in somehow. I later discovered that he would sometimes sit outside the interview room. I was aware that Steve was a Freemason but I had little idea what that actually meant. Over the years since then I've wondered if any of his brothers at the Lodge had anything to do with the fact that the case went nowhere. I'm no conspiracy theorist but when I read the police records decades later and discovered that the videos of my interviews had mysteriously gone missing, I really had to wonder.

My mother's behaviour grew increasingly bizarre. She was puzzlingly spiteful, even going so far as to forbid me to take any of my personal belongings from my room, which I found devastating. Treasured items, including my old teddy bear Bruno, who had been a constant companion since my days in Trelech, were kept from me for no logical reason. Aside from this unmotivated meanness, she also did and said some really strange things that placed her sanity in serious question. For example, it was revealed that Steve had made her pregnant too at some point during the past three years. When asked to confirm that she had both aborted the child and had a hysterectomy, she acknowledged the former but vehemently denied the latter, as if that was an affront to her feminine dignity somehow. She also manipulated every interview so that it became all about her. Then when Christmas came, she made sure to send me a gift: lacy underwear! In retrospect, I can see that she wasn't in her right mind – perhaps never had been – but I didn't have that understanding at the time. Her actions were just incomprehensibly cruel, a terrible betrayal. She had never been a loving mother but I still had no reason to expect that she would act like this.

A new routine set in: school, home to my foster family while also avoiding Steve, regular check-ins with the social workers and police, asking if I could collect my belongings, hearing that the answer was no, and so on, and so on – and debating where I was going to live of course.

My foster mother cared more about the income from Social Services than my wellbeing. Day in, day out, I ate nothing but jam sandwiches and sat alone in my room. I found myself thinking of the simple pleasures of my life in Trelech. We would go to the market in the village sometimes to buy fresh produce. I used to love nothing more than the peaches sold there and I would use the money my grandmother regularly sent me to buy them. I longed for one of them now. Such a small, simple thing to miss, yet somehow representative of so much that I had lost.

As for my dad, I actually had no idea what he had to say about all this. With me in foster care, he stepped forward to take my brother into his custody but somehow that never happened. He later said that he would take me in permanently as well. I was never privy to any of the conversations the social workers had with him but according to their report, he seemed to feel extremely guilty. Well he might, I suppose, but his guilt wasn't much use to me.

There isn't too much more to say about that time of suspended uncertainty. No sooner had I found my way out of my nightmare than I seemed to find myself in a lingering bad dream where I was stuck in quicksand or sticky marshland that sucked my feet in every time I tried to take a step forward. When decision time finally came, I was forced to do what I had been accused of doing: lie – or, at the very least, omit a crucial truth that would have changed everything.

"How would you feel about living with your dad?" The social worker spoke in her usual soft, pleasant voice, trying to seem casual, yet with her sharp, unwavering stare, betraying the fact that she was probing for an answer to a vitally important question.

"Yeah, that would be fine."

"How do you like it when you visit your dad?"

"It's great. I've missed the horses. It would be so nice to see them every day."

"Do you get on with your dad?"

I nodded.

"What do you think it would be like if you lived with him?"

She was approaching the point in a broadly roundabout way but it was very clear, even to my thirteen-year-old mind, what she was driving at.

"I would really like that," I said.

She decided to get to the point: "Your dad's never hurt you in any way…?"

The thought was almost funny to me. Despite all the times I had seen my Dad beat my mother, I had never regarded him as anything but completely harmless where I was concerned. I shook my head.

"Wendy, I have to ask: your mum has said some things about your dad…"

I simply stared back at her blankly, feigning ignorance.

"Have you ever seen your dad being violent?"

I shook my head again. No doubt, my mother had said many things over the past few months. This woman and her colleagues had every reason to be doubtful of her wild, disjointed declarations, which mixed fact with fabrication and outright delusion. I barely even had to lie; all I had to do was allow everyone to confirm for themselves the doubts they already had. It had to be done – what was the alternative? If I confessed to witnessing brutal beatings as a child, I was convinced that I would be stuck in my miserable foster home forever and that was not an option for me.

"So you think you would be happy and safe at your dad's?"

"Of course."

"Well, he's offered to take you to go and live with him permanently."

"When can I go?"

So that's how I ended up living in a tumbledown lodge in Wales with ghosts and horses for company. Only a small step, but a step nonetheless. One step closer to my vision of a happier life, which still somehow burned intensely inside me, getting clearer and stronger with every move.

*

The social workers had feared that if I did move in with Dad, I would end up being nothing more than a live-in maid. As it turned out, there were strong grounds for that fear. If there was cooking and cleaning to be done, I was the one doing it. But I didn't mind. It felt good to be in a position to bring order and cleanliness. Since I was very young, I had loved keeping things tidy, making to-do lists and ticking off the tasks as I went. I suppose that, for a life that was so out of control in so many ways, I took whatever opportunity I could to exert order and structure. Both were sorely needed at Dad's house at the old lodge. Although he was still with Lisa, with whom I got on quite well – probably because she was closer to my age than Dad's – the place was essentially a bachelor pad. It needed a feminine touch and I was happy to provide it.

Cooking duties were something that filled me with stress. It still makes me anxious, even to this day. With the first few meals I cooked there I was painfully aware of an episode from the early days in Trelech. My mother had made custard one day and my Dad had complained that it was cold and lumpy. He was so angry at her lack of culinary skill that he flung the bowl at her. It had struck her hard on the shin and shattered, sending earthenware fragments and blood-splattered custard across the room. There was a deadly silence as he stormed out of the room and my mother sat with blood dripping from her leg. With that anecdote always at the front of my mind, I was terribly eager to please my Dad when it came to food preparation. He had a way of heightening the tension for me because I would finish cooking and have the food ready to serve, and call him, wherever he was – usually in his workshop – but he would never come straightaway. I would go into apoplexy worrying how he would react if he came to eat and found the food cold. At the time, I didn't know how to reheat food without ruining it. Thankfully, my fears were ungrounded. Dad never showed me anything but gratitude as far as my efforts in the kitchen were concerned.

Compared to where I had been, this life was a pleasure. Sure, I had to keep house and help take care of the horses, but aside from that, I was a free agent. There was no Steve to worry about and no constant tension with my mother. Dad left me to my own devices and that was exactly what I needed. The years that were to follow ended up being a kind of recovery period for me, a respite from what had gone before, with plenty of time for introspection. It wasn't as though all wounds were healed. It would be years before that would happen. Dad was far from an ideal father but he had taken me out of a toxic situation and given me a chance for something resembling normality. I can thank him for that much at least. If only he had thought to do so a few years earlier.

The biggest worry was that my brother hadn't come with me. My mother had surrendered custody of me but she refused to release him. So the two of us grew up apart from each other. Life had taken a difficult turn for him and my mother after I left. Steve broke off the relationship and promptly kicked both of them out of his house. It took some time before they could find their feet again. I was relieved that my brother was out of Steve's shadow but I still worried about my mother's influence.

As for Steve, he was out of my life now but I know that I was not the first girl he had done this to. And thanks to my mother, I'm sure I wasn't the last.

Except where my mother was concerned, Dad was not a

confrontational person at all. He never once mentioned anything about Steve or what he had done. Not a word. From his point of view, it was probably best not to dwell on such nasty subjects. To this day, I still don't know what my Dad thought of the fact that his daughter had been treated as a sex toy for three years. Was he angry? Was he sad? Or, as his actions seemed to demonstrate, did he not really care? I had no way of knowing. That was just how he was.

One of the benefits of being at Dad's was that I could be involved with the horses again – something I had genuinely enjoyed in my younger years and had missed. I loved grooming them, riding them, feeding them, going to all the shows. However, there was a downside to the horsey world as well. Dad had a number of friends in that arena who were also friends of Steve's. I remember John, for example, who insisted that my Dad not bring me into his house because of the 'terrible lies' I had told about Steve. Dad passively obliged. Whenever he went to John's and I happened to be with him, I had to wait in the car, out in the cold with no heater to keep me warm. I didn't object. It upset me, but it made sense to me; the way I saw it, a girl like me would never be properly accepted.

Then there was Philip, another friend of both Steve and Dad's, who invited me into his horsebox to show me the puppies his dog had just given birth to – and then took the opportunity to feel me up. I told Dad what had happened, and he laughed it off, saying something like, "Yeah, you have to be careful with him; he's like that."

On one occasion, we were invited to a particularly posh party, which was quite an important event in the local equestrian community. While Dad went and socialised with his friends and colleagues, I hung around the bar, where a young barman took a shine to me and started to ply me with drinks. It wasn't my first time drinking – I was a regular drinker by the age of fourteen – but I had never had this much. How much did I drink? I'm not sure exactly but it was enough for me to end the night passed out in the ladies' room. I didn't remember anything of what happened at the time, but I later had flashbacks of being carried out of the toilet kicking and screaming. "You don't know what it's like to be raped! Do you know how many times I've been raped? Hundreds and hundreds of times!"

As might be expected, the episode was never mentioned by me or Dad. One thing's for sure: I wasn't invited to any more high society parties after that.

There was no pocket money from Dad, so I looked around for any opportunity to work for a bit of cash. I didn't live in the kind of area where I could just head down to the nearest mall or high street and see which chain store or boutique was hiring. My options were limited to the hotel several miles up the road from home. When I wasn't at school, I would go there during the day and clean. I spent the daylight hours there tidying the chalets and scrubbing toilets and then, when night fell and the kitchen opened, I took off my rubber gloves, washed up and shifted into waitress mode, carrying drinks and plates of food around until the place closed at night. The last thing I wanted to do when I got home was prepare dinner – and our kitchen wasn't very well stocked anyway – so I would make up my evening meal with leftovers off customers' plates. Then I would walk out onto the road and – against my better judgment – thumb a ride back home.

I didn't mind any of this. On the contrary, I relished it because I knew it was all leading somewhere. These were just small, incremental advances towards the life I wanted – a life that I was going to get on my own and on my terms. With every toilet I scrubbed, with each plate I served or scraped, I had my mind set on the life I would one day have. My dream of some day living somewhere hot and foreign, far away from the gloom I had known all my life, never left me. In fact, its focus sharpened, with little details being added each time I thought about it. I knew that soon I was going to travel, meet lots of interesting people and have many adventures. So this was a small price to pay. People who haven't had to mop floors, clean restrooms and move glasses and plates around for patrons of all dispositions and varying levels of sobriety, or do similar menial jobs, can never know the sense of satisfaction that comes with pocketing those notes at the end of the night, knowing that this is just the start, that it can only get better, that there's so much more in store.

Of course, I would be lying if I said I was happy and focused on my future every day. There were plenty of bad days when the hurt, the bad memories, the loneliness, the shame and humiliation, seemed likely to swallow me whole, regardless of any vision or positive thoughts. It seems a bit perverse, but what actually kept me going through those dark days was knowing that, if I didn't find my dreams, if things didn't get better, I always had the option to end my life. I had tried it before and it had actually been quite simple. It hadn't worked that time but the next time I could try harder, I would take more tablets or find a more conclusive method. Death was not something to be frightened of; it was a comfort. A kind of 'fail safe' measure in case all other plans fell apart.

I can't remember at what point it was during my stay with Dad that Lisa decided to leave him for another man. He was absolutely devastated. For weeks, I would lie in bed at night and hear him crying himself to sleep. It was probably the most emotion I ever saw him show. Dad was not someone who could stay single for long and he was soon signed up to a dating service. New girlfriends came and went. Within a short period, I went from shutting out the sounds of his weeping at night, to cringing through the sounds of loud sex. I can't remember how many there were. Ultimately, Jenny came along and, for reasons I couldn't understand, passed whatever tests my Dad had for long-term relationship material. Within three weeks, she had moved in and after two months, they were engaged to be married.

Jenny hated me for no apparent reason, and the feeling was mutual. Even on the day of their wedding – a small, simple celebration at the local pub – I knew without a doubt that we couldn't stay together in the same house for very long. She had a son, a few years older than me, who would sometimes come and stay with us. I didn't like him either; there was something deeply unpleasant about his whole air and attitude. My Dad, however, did nothing but sing his praises.

One weekend, Dad and Jenny went away, and left me alone with this person who, technically I suppose, was my stepbrother. I just did my best to give him a wide berth. As I often did when Dad was away, I invited some friends around and hosted a party. Among these was a girl who had become my best friend since I had moved back to Wales. We all had a great time, despite the presence of my obnoxious stepbrother. Once the party had died down and everyone but Jenny's son, my best friend and I had left; I headed upstairs to my bedroom. He went off to bed and my friend made herself comfortable on the couch in the lounge. I woke up in the small hours to the muffled sounds of some kind of commotion downstairs. I ran down to investigate and found that Jenny's delightful son had raped my best friend! I was traumatised and enraged on her behalf. I carried her shame and pain for years.

Based on Dad's track record, I should have known what sort of response I would get from him when I told him what had happened while he and Jenny were away.

"Well," he said, "she does have a bit of a reputation, you know. She likes the boys."

This friend of mine had taught me something extremely valuable. During my years at Dad's house, the bad dreams I had started having years back had become habitual and they had shifted shape slightly as well. In Aldershot, I used to have recurring nightmares in which I was being raped. I would scream and scream but no sound would come out. The screams were completely silent, like the ones I was suppressing throughout my three years of horror. Once I got to Dad's place, the dreams evolved. Now the screams weren't silent anymore. My voice rang out loudly in terror and rage. In these new versions of the dream, however, it was my arms and legs that wouldn't respond. I would try to fight, but was completely paralysed.

Until my friend offered me some excellent advice, these dreams had plagued me most nights. She taught me how to wake myself up and pull myself out of the nightmares. Perhaps she knew this because she had had similar night-time experiences. I never thought it possible before; my experience had always been that the dream would just happen and I would be helpless to resist it. I would have to go along with it until it let me go. Over the years, though, I learned to perfect the art of mastering my dreams and drawing myself up into wakefulness before the terror took hold. That was thanks to her. It was an important revelation because it showed me that we need not just accept the circumstances in which we find ourselves. If we can master the art of taking control in the midst of a dream, how much more power do we have in waking life?

I think I was angrier at Dad's response to the attack that had happened under his own roof, than I was at his lack of reaction when the same thing was happening to me. I was actually disappointed, though I should have known better than to expect anything else. That was the final nail in the coffin of any real relationship with Dad – and it wouldn't be long before I was out from under his roof. Jenny wanted me gone as soon as possible and Dad made no attempt to counter her unwelcoming attitude, so I was happy to oblige.

I was just about to finish my O-levels and I had my mind set on heading off to college. With my vision of a tropical paradise still clear in my mind, I had decided to study travel and tourism. That seemed to me to be the easiest way to start seeing the world. I enrolled at the Swansea Institute of Higher Learning, which was offering the perfect course. So the time came when Jenny – not Dad – packed me and my things into her car and took me away as fast as she could. I don't remember if Dad even said goodbye – he certainly didn't check to see that I had everything I needed. He wasn't paying for anything and he hadn't even questioned how I would be covering my costs.

I was barely sixteen years old and my life as a dependent was over. I was truly on my own now. The world awaited and although doubt, fear and shame still plagued me, I reached out to embrace it with both hands.

CHAPTER FIVE: FROM SWANSEA TO BRIGHTON

"Every goal that has ever been reached began with just one step – and the belief that it could be attained. When the road becomes hard to travel and it feels as if you'll never reach the end... look deep inside your heart and you will find strength you never knew you had. Believe in yourself – and remember that dreams really can come true."

– Jason Blume

I arrived in the city of Swansea with nothing more than a suitcase and with no money except what little I had saved from my cleaning and waitressing job. I found a local paper and searched for accommodation. Soon I was set up in a tiny bedroom in a house in quite a nice, upmarket part of town, known for its student housing. Oddly enough, despite the pleasant neighbourhood, my room was just upstairs from what was essentially a drug den. It wasn't much but it was mine for now – and I would have to find a way to pay for it.

Work was relatively easy to come by. Within a week of my arrival, I had been recruited by a double-glazing company as a salesperson. In the afternoons after college and on weekends, I would go door to door trying to convince residents that what their homes needed were doubled-glazed windows. As it turned out though, I wouldn't have much time to master the subtle of art of window marketing. I had only been there about a month when my boss approached me with the opportunity to make some extra money on the side. He offered me fifty pounds – a massive amount of money for me in those days – if I would pose for some photographs for him. I didn't stop to consider what the content of the photos would be. All I knew was that it was an incredible fifty pounds for maybe about an hour's work. It was too good a proposition to pass up and I agreed.

So, one afternoon, I found myself going to my boss's house with him. Looking back, especially considering everything I had gone through, it was an incredibly reckless thing to do. Despite it all, I was still very naïve. Was it the unconscious belief that lightning couldn't strike twice, so to speak? I had been taken advantage of multiple times in the past. Surely it wouldn't happen again? Had my previous trauma desensitised me and conditioned me not to fear the worst? Or was it simply a case of the allure of much-needed rent money overriding my better judgement? Whatever it was, I made the decision to go with him. It was only when the front door shut behind us that the potential risk of the situation really occurred to me. The feeling I had six years earlier, when Steve's front door had shut me into a living hell, suddenly returned. "Oh my God," I thought. "What the hell am I doing here?"

More alarm bells started to ring when he took me to his daughter's bedroom and asked me to sit on the bed, which was covered with teddy bears. He was never angry or abusive, never tried to force me to do anything. He very calmly told me what he wanted, which was to take off my top and pose with the stuffed toys in various positions. I had very few inhibitions about nudity – my life with Steve had quickly worn away any such modesty. It's not that I would volunteer to strip off in front of a stranger, but if it ever came to it, I felt, what would it matter? So taking off my top was a small thing to ask. Perhaps, I thought, as I undressed, this was all I was worth anyway. Just as Steve had often said, this is all men would want from me; it all made sense. I wonder now, when I think about it, what made this man target me? Do predators leave their mark so that others like them can identify fair game? Or was I somehow subconsciously advertising that I was damaged goods and could be had at a discount?

I don't know how long it took. I did all I was asked to do – sitting, lying, stuffed toys suggestively positioned as directed. As he took the photos, I could clearly see his erection pushing against the inside of his trousers. Thankfully, this situation did not turn out as badly as it could have. Once he was happy that he had all the shots he wanted, I put my clothes back on, then he gave me my fifty pounds and took me back home. He asked if we could do it again the following week and hinted that maybe we could do something more. I took the money and ran – and didn't return to work the next day. A dark thought occurred to me though: men would be willing to pay me to do things like this, everything from posing for pictures to actual sex. How easy it would be to make money – and it would be far more than any bartending or waitressing job could provide. Thankfully, I was not so far gone as to give in to these thoughts. I still knew, deep down, that I deserved better than that – but this would not be the last time that I would entertain the idea. In the face of hunger and the need to keep a roof over one's head, even the strongest of wills can start to buckle.

One day it became too much and I did what I swore I would never do. I went into a phone booth outside the college and I dialled Dad's number. I had been determined never to ask for help but my rent was due and I was starving. As fate would have it, he didn't answer the phone – Jenny did.

"Hi, Jenny. It's Wendy."

"Oh… Hello." I could feel the dislike and resentment emanating from her, coming towards me down the phone line, hanging thick in the space between us.

"Is Dad there?"

"He can't come to the phone. He's busy at the moment. We've got a lot to do now with the move and all."

"What move?"

"Oh, has he not told you? We're moving to France."

No, he hadn't told me – and evidently had no intention of doing so – or it simply hadn't occurred to him. It would be a year before he would even call me to check if I was okay. I had always known that I was on my own but I thought I could at least call on him in an emergency. After that day, I decided I would never even try again. I don't remember how I managed to pay rent and get fed but I made a plan – and swore I would continue to do so from then on.

Someone told me that I was entitled to government housing benefit, which had never occurred to me before. At least, with that, I wouldn't have to worry about rent anymore. However, I put in the application only to find out that I did not qualify because I had been declared a ward of the court after I was removed from Steve and my mother's house. If I was struggling to pay for accommodation, I was told, the only option was to be moved into another foster home until I was eighteen. I refused to even consider that option, so I decided I would have to just struggle along on my own. I would find a way. I had come this far, I certainly wasn't about to give up now.

With my double-glazing job now gone, I had to find something else. I soon replaced it with, not one, but two new positions. I would be in classes until early afternoon and then I would go to work as a telemarketer for a photographic studio. I was given a phone, a script and a list of numbers that I would spend the next four hours working through. I would knock that off at eight o'clock and head to Tasty Bites, where I would serve kebabs and other fast food to night owls and drunken revellers until around two or three in the morning. Then I would head home, go to bed and do it all again. In between, I had to find time to study and complete my projects. On average, I was getting by on about three or four hours of sleep a night.

It was hard work but of all the "wash-rinse-repeat" daily routines I had gone through so far in my life, this was absolutely the best. Never before had I experienced such independence, such empowerment. With my two jobs, my studies and my living arrangements, there was a lot to manage and somehow I succeeded, despite being only sixteen years old. It was not easy and I really shouldn't have needed to be so independent at that age. Nevertheless, it was during my Swansea years that I really discovered my innate self-sufficiency. With each passing day, I was proving to myself how capable I was of building and sustaining my life without support from anyone. I was training my independence and ingenuity like developing muscles, getting stronger all the time.

Some people believe that at points in your life when you start to feel real positive change, the universe conspires to test you. Events and people arise in your life to poke and prod at what you're building, to check just how sound the structure really is. If they find holes, they teach you the lessons required to fill them. If the foundation you've built is solid, then the trials presented by these people and events have a minimal effect. In my case, my rapidly developing independent drive for success, and the self-esteem I was repairing by slow degrees, were about to undergo a major test – one that would take me years to pass.

It started with what I thought would be an ordinary shift at Tasty Bites, about a year after I had moved to Swansea. It had been a fairly busy night and every customer started to look the same as every other to me, but then one walked in who stood out among the crowd. He was in incredible shape and was the most immaculately dressed man I had ever seen in my life. I didn't have much dress sense at the time; I had an unconscious and practical approach to clothing that came from years of wearing hand-me-downs. I wore whatever I had and didn't think too much about fashion. Yet even I could see that this person was on another level. There was not a hair or a thread out of place. He was also clearly someone who exercised a lot and he was careful to show off the results of his efforts in an obvious but tasteful way. He exuded confidence and charm and what's more, he took notice of me. I was flattered and completely disarmed by the attention this older man, who looked as if he had just walked off a movie set, was showing me. By the time he came in, I was greasy and tired and ready to get home, shower and fall into bed. Yet here was this man, who could probably have any girl he wanted, showing interest in me.

That's how Darel came into my life.

Eight years my elder, he seemed the opposite of me in every way. Whereas my poor fashion and social sense were plain for all to see, he appeared sophisticated, a real man of the world. At seventeen, I was pushing myself to make my mark on the world, sweating daily to prove myself scholastically and financially. He had the air of someone who had already made it, who had it all worked out. While I had never had anything even close to a serious relationship yet, he was already a father of three. Also, to me with my English roots and rural Welsh upbringing, his West Indian heritage seemed exotic and alluring. How little I knew about the world: in a short time, I would realise that he was not confident, he did not have anything made, and his powerful and sculpted physique covered a fragile ego that was weaker, more lost and more afraid than I would ever be.

By this time, since I had first arrived in Swansea, I had moved a number of times. I left the first place as soon as I possibly could after an experience at the drug den downstairs. One day, I decided to go down there and allowed myself to be convinced to take a drag or two from a bong that was being passed around. I promptly passed out. Later I decided that this wasn't the kind of environment I wanted to be in and moved to much nicer student quarters, eventually finding my way up to the attic room, which I had had my eye on since I first walked into the house. I spent my first Christmas Day in Swansea alone in that room, eating cabbage and beans, with a dessert of cheap biscuits. I had never felt so alone as I looked out of my window at the wintry cityscape. Dad was in France, I didn't know where my mother and brother were, and all my fellow students had gone home to their families. I was not aware then of the statistical fact that the majority of suicides in the Western world happen on Christmas Day, but if someone had told me that, I would have understood completely.

I started to wonder what would happen if I made another

attempt to end it all, and succeeded. Would anyone even notice? My housemates would only be back after New Year's and they would find me long gone. I might be dead already for all my Dad knew. I could literally disappear and nobody would think anything of it.

A few months later, Darel came along and things moved very quickly. Within two months of meeting, we had moved in together. At least I wouldn't be alone next Christmas. I found it easier then to pick up my moods and feel optimistic about the future. Not only was I a good student and a hardworking, self-sustaining adult, I was also in a serious relationship. Darel didn't work much and I didn't give much thought to how he was making a living. He would work a few nights a week as a bouncer at the clubs nearby. He wasn't much of a drinker so we seldom partied very hard. We just enjoyed each other's company, often simply watching movies at home together or going out to the cinema.

Towards the end of my final year in college, things took a decisive turn in an unexpected direction. It started when a friend of Darel's introduced him to Ecstasy. He soon roped me in with his stories of how incredible the experience was. I tried it and found that he wasn't wrong – the feeling of euphoria, the increased energy, the deep sense of joy and connection. It made it so easy for me to block out painful memories from my past – or even unpleasant thoughts about my current situation. Before long, it was all we wanted to do over the weekends. By this time, I was working in a clothing store – part-time at first, and then full-time after I had finished my studies. I would work there from Monday to Friday. Then we would go out, hit the pills, and party non-stop all throughout the weekend.

That went on for longer than I care to admit. Soon we added cocaine into the mix as well. I won't lie and say that I wasn't enjoying myself. I knew though that there was a risk that this life could suck me in and I would be stuck in it forever – and I was simply not prepared to allow that to happen. I would go off with Darel on crazy, weekend-long benders but I never lost sight of the fact that I was working towards something. When Monday morning arrived, I was back in the game. I knew the time was coming when I would be walking away from Swansea, because I did not see my future in this little isolated corner of Wales. I had a world to see and I had decided that my first step would be Brighton. There I planned to work for American Express – the British head office was based there – and that would be my jumping off point for the travel I had in mind. Darel was not particularly interested in this idea; he seemed happy where he was and his lack of ambition and adventure was starting to irritate me. I decided to end it with him and be on my way. He convinced me not to break it off, however, agreeing to come with me to Brighton. Eventually we decided that I would go ahead and he would follow.

I managed to secure an interview with American Express through a temping agency. The day of my interview was a memorable one because I had managed to catch a bout of food poisoning. Feeling seriously under the weather, and constantly running to and from the restroom, I still insisted on pushing through. Illness simply wasn't an option. I made it through that day on sheer willpower, and they hired me on a trial basis. Within a few months, I was a permanent employee.

It's incredible how everything in Brighton just seemed to fall into place. I landed the exact job I was hoping for, and my boss, Nigel, ended up becoming a close friend. Our friendship was firmly established when we decided to go flat hunting together. Every year, since before I was thirteen – when I had finally revealed the truth about Steve – I had set a particular goal for myself to reach by my next birthday. This arose from the life-changing disaster of my tenth birthday. As I remembered that terrible day, I committed to making sure that every birthday from then on would mark a decisive, positive step forward. I arrived in Brighton with my eighteenth birthday just around the corner and I set myself the goal of owning my first property as soon as that milestone came. Nigel was also in the market for a new flat, so we decided to search together. We met at Preston Park Station, even snapping a photograph of ourselves there before we set off – long before the days of selfies, I might add. Together we found just the place – one for me and one for him, right across the road from one another. I was eighteen years and one week old, and I was granted my first mortgage and became a property owner. It was nothing more than a little basement flat but I was more proud of it than I'd ever been of anything in my life.

Darel inspected the place and sneered: "It will do for a year or so."
We ended up staying there for seven years. He resented the fact that
it was mine and talked a big game about finding a new place, which
he never actually did. He claimed to want something that was in his
own name but never had the drive to go out and get it. I supported us
through those years, first with my job at American Express, and then
two other posts that I moved onto after that. Darel never took any
kind of formal work at any point in Brighton. He managed to find
occasional work as a bouncer and later graduated from being a drug
user to a dealer. I was too young and naïve to realise that what he was
doing was sponging off me.

I would never have been able to support us both had it not been for
the lucrative side-line we got going. We managed to get mortgages
on a number of properties, which we then rented out as student
accommodation. Together with my salary, as well as the rental we
received from our numerous properties, we were able to cover the
mortgage instalments and then finally, we got a decent passive income
going. If we had used that money wisely we could have set ourselves
up for life. Darel felt that this was all he needed; he didn't have to
work. My argument was that I was part of that business too but I was
still working. I still went to my job, regardless of the rental income. If
we were both working then the rental income could be saved and not
lived off. Needless to say, he didn't see it that way.

I later discovered that Darel had secured our mortgages through the back door, so to speak. He had an insider in the local building society to whom he would slip two hundred pounds to ensure that the mortgage was approved. It was all above board aside from that – I was extremely conscientious about the mortgage payments. However, Darel's business habits were still a massive red flag that I should have taken note of. Why didn't I? Because, at the time, I could see no alternative to him. He was who he was, and he was in my life and I had to take the good with the bad, because how could a girl like me find anyone better?

If you thought that I had abandoned my hard partying, snorting and pill popping when I got to Brighton, I'm sorry to say you're very wrong. We were more into that lifestyle than we had been in Swansea and somehow I very successfully managed to live a double life – an art I had mastered during my three years in Steve's house. If any of my colleagues and supervisors at the three companies I worked for in Brighton had heard what I got up to over the weekend, they would have been shocked. From Monday to Friday I was the perfect corporate employee. But when the weekend came, it was as if I flicked a switch, which I would then turn off again when Monday morning came around.

Darel was even more locked into the drug lifestyle than I was and because he had more time on his hands, he used the substances a lot more often than I did. I don't think the Ecstasy had that much of a lasting effect on either of us but as Darel's cocaine habit took hold, things headed downhill fast.

How did I not see any of the signs, I think to myself now? How did it go on for so long? At one point, I discovered that Darel hadn't been paying the mortgage on one of the properties, which was ultimately repossessed. From that point on, I took over the management of the houses myself. So now, I was working and managing all the properties while he sat back and collected his part of the revenue.

I brought up the question of children quite often. I so wanted to be a mother. For Darel though, eight years older and already the father of three children – actually a fourth child came to light not long after we met – it really wasn't a priority. This was another warning sign I should have seen. Darel made no attempt to support his children, financially or otherwise. I was the one who bought and sent the annual Christmas and birthday cards.

He insisted that we needed to be married first and he was in no hurry to make that happen - it was just a stalling tactic. "I'll have to think about it," he'd say. I know women who would have walked out instantly at a response like that. But for me, this was as good as it got. How could I walk away? I really did love him – and what if there was nobody better out there? His family was another deterrent I should have taken note of. His mother hated me – I think because she saw me as a little girl who was distracting her son from the life he should be leading – and the children he should be raising. I'll never forget the day that she and Darel's sister came into the clothing store I used to work at back in Swansea – for no better reason than to make fun of the low class shop-girl their precious son and brother had taken up with. Then there was our first New Year "celebration" after we met. We took the drive to London, where his sister lived, to celebrate with his family. However, why I went along, I don't even know; of course I was not welcome. Darel parked the car outside his sister's house and then went inside to enjoy the New Year's festivities. What did I do, you ask? Nothing I hadn't done before; I sat in the car in the cold and waited for them to finish, feeling the familiar feelings of being alone and unloved.

This is one of those dark, deceptive moments of confirmation we sometimes have in our lives – especially those of us who struggle with our self-esteem and are already convinced that nobody really loves us, that there is really no place in the world where we belong. That is how I felt deep down, and as I sat there, seething with impotent rage, I remembered Dad leaving me in the car while he was inside with his girlfriend, or asking me stay outside while he visited John, who didn't want me in his house. It was clear confirmation of what I already suspected about my value – or lack of value. It was unjust, but… well… it was me. That's how life was, wasn't it? For girls like me, anyway.

However, underneath the anger and the self-pity, there was something else. That little voice spoke in my head. That vision burgeoned in my mind's eye. That powerful, self-assured part of me quietly reminded me that this was not it. This was not what I deserved, nor all my life would ever be. That voice wasn't loud at that point, it was overpowered by the negativity of the moment, but it was still clear enough to make itself heard and to offer a convincing promise that one day it would be in full song and I wouldn't hear anything else

I didn't know when that was going to happen, but I knew it would.

CHAPTER SIX: DOMESTIC BLISS

S o I stayed with Darel – and the worst and craziest was yet to come. I was content with things as they were; I had experienced far worse and I had no precedent in my life that could inspire me to expect anything better. I was so sure this was all I was going to get that I went so far as to relieve him of the responsibility of proposing. What was the point in waiting? Nobody was ever going to propose to me; I was never going to get my fairy tale engagement. I thought I might as well just take the matter into my own hands as I had everything else.

I asked him – and he said yes – and then he backtracked a couple of times. "I'll have to think about it," he kept saying. The interesting thing was that, at the beginning, marriage was more something he wanted than I did. I had broached the subject of children and he had insisted that if we were to have children, we would need to be married first. As having children was vitally important to me, I seriously considered marriage. By the time I proposed, I was excited for the future.

Ultimately, I suppose when he felt he had kept me hanging long enough and had wrestled sufficient control of the situation away from me, he agreed. The wedding was on. Even if I was paying for it, I was going to have my special day. My marriage was set to begin in a sunny, foreign destination I had only imagined up to this point. I had no idea then that, a few years later, it would end in another.

Since a large part of Darel's extended family lived in Jamaica, we thought it would be a wonderful idea to have the wedding there. We – or I, at least – had saved up the money. I recalled the fantasy destination I had been imagining since I was a little girl and dared to hope that I may just be on the verge of seeing it for real.

Because of the costs involved, it would be a relatively small wedding party. Nobody from my family would be coming, with the exception of my brother, with whom I had thankfully re-established a relationship a short while before. We didn't really know each other very well, and were in the process of re-building a relationship, so his presence there meant a great deal to me. Aside from him, all the other guests were from Darel's family. I had invited Dad but he declined. By this time, his marriage to Jenny had fallen apart and he had a new partner to take up his attention. He had also just moved from France to Ireland and I certainly wasn't a priority in his life just then. It appeared I never had been.

By this time, Darel's parents had completely changed their attitude towards me. They had started to thaw when I was still back in Swansea. It happened the day I went around to the house, knocked on the door and confronted his mother, shortly after she and his sister had shown up at the shop just to make fun of me. I was emboldened by the fact that I would soon be moving cities, and wouldn't be seeing them very often, so didn't have anything to lose. I told her that I was not going to stand being treated like that. I explained that I was constantly telling Darel that he should spend time with his kids and that his absence from their lives had nothing to do with me, and I certainly wasn't to be blamed for what happened in the past, before I had even entered the picture. After that, she did a hundred-and-eighty-degree turn. Being a devout Christian, she began to describe me as some sort of angel that had been sent into their lives. By the time the wedding came, she was thrilled to have me as a daughter-in-law. She even made my dress – a dress fit for a princess.

We arrived in Kingston, Jamaica and I fell in love with the Caribbean. The wedding was to be a beach affair at a posh resort. As I got ready, being dressed, pampered, and made up like royalty, I had to keep looking around me to make sure it was all real. How far I had come from Trelech.

Darel had different priorities though. One of the first items on his to-do list was to stock up on coke – and lots of it. I wasn't really conscious of it at the time, because I was partaking as well, but Darel had formed a dangerous habit by this time. He used coke virtually every day in fairly copious quantities. In addition to the steroids he took to keep himself bulked up, the cocaine was having a strange effect on his character. He suffered from delusions and he would sometimes dream up the most ridiculous schemes. He started talking to himself, and at times, he could get frighteningly aggressive. On our wedding night, he was in an exuberant mood but he was absolutely in a world of his own. I had previously had visions of consummating our marriage, of being made love to, madly and passionately, for the first time as a wife. For someone who equated sex so closely with love, as I did in the depths of my wounded psyche, which had been so twisted and manipulated in my formative years, this was extremely important to me.

As I lay back on the lavishly decorated bed in the bridal suite, still wearing the wedding dress my new mother-in-law had made for me. I stretched luxuriously, feeling every bit the princess. Who would have thought this day would ever come? The fact that I had arranged it all myself gave me all the more reason to revel in this day and everything that came with it. Being the princess that I was, I turned my gaze to my loving prince.

My prince did not see me. He was staring wide-eyed into space and grinding his teeth, muttering quietly to himself. Then he sat down at the dressing table and busied himself chopping more lines of coke. Well that was that. We would not be consummating our marriage that night. I should have known, of course. Cocaine always anaesthetised his sex drive. He was only interested in partying now, probably right up until we had to board the flight back home. I felt a sting of rejection.

He was chattering on about some or other nightclub that his cousins had been talking about, pausing only long enough to take half a line up each nostril. Then he turned and offered me some. I looked at the mirror he was holding out in one hand and the cut-off plastic straw in the other – much more efficient than the rolled-up banknote you see in the movies. I gave it a moment's thought, feeling resentment boiling up, and pushing it down.

Oh well, if you can't beat them… I sat up and took what was offered.

That was how the after-party of our Jamaican wedding kicked off. The rest of the celebrations are a bit of a blur now. The flight home felt like the longest one in history as I quickly crashed back to everyday reality after the most extended coke binge I had ever been on. There were moments when I honestly thought I was going to die or my face would fall off. My nose throbbed, my head ached and my jaw was in agony.

I never thought I would be so happy to see the front door of my humble flat in Brighton. I walked in and threw myself on the bed, ready to sleep for as many hours as it took to get this out of my system. I would have expected Darel to do the same but he went straight for his suitcase. "Is he unpacking now?" I wondered. No, not exactly, it turned out. He reached into his bag, pulled out his stash of coke and started chopping lines again. He had actually brought it back with him from Jamaica – just packed it in his checked luggage! How it got through security at both Norman Manley and Heathrow Airports I will never know.

After the effects of the wedding festivities died down, life in Brighton got back into its normal routine. Well, not quite normal. I started to notice that things were off when I would go into the kitchen and find that all the burners on the gas stove had been left on at their maximum. When I asked Darel why he had left them on, he looked at me as if I was speaking a foreign language. On other occasions, I would hear him talking in another room. When I went to see who he was talking to, I would find him sitting alone, chatting animatedly to himself.

If I was tempted to pass these incidents off as minor, our next trip to London should have pushed all doubts aside and raised the alarm loud and clear. We were driving to see his brother one Saturday, me behind the wheel and him in the passenger seat. We were about twenty minutes into the northward trip along the M23 when Darel said something I could not quite make out.

"What?" I asked.

He was facing towards the backseat and turned to look at me with mild irritation as if I had interrupted a conversation he was having. He turned his head back towards the rear and spoke again. Obviously, I was extremely confused – there was nobody in the backseat. When I asked what he was talking about, he looked at me in confusion, then turned to face the front and fell silent. A few minutes later, I was nearly deafened by the "whoosh" sound of wind rushing into the car and could actually feel the vehicle buck slightly to one side as the passenger side door flew open. We were travelling at around 80mph. My shouts were smothered by the sound of the rushing air. Cars were whizzing by us on both sides, I was not able to move over to the shoulder so I could stop. Finally he pulled the door shut again, bristling at my angry, fear-filled shouts. Darel had just opened the car door whilst travelling!

I was shaken and, concerned about his state of mind. I decided I was not going to carry on with this 90-minute trip, since he was likely to get us killed. I took the next exit and turned around, heading straight back to Brighton. He didn't even notice until I pulled into the parking space at our flat. Then, when he realised that we were back in Brighton instead of London, he flew into an epic rage the likes of which I had never seen.

He demanded the car keys, saying that he would simply go to London without me. I knew that he would only cause an accident and possibly end up dead, so I refused. I can only imagine what our neighbours must have thought, to see this heavily muscled man screaming at the top of his voice with absolutely unbridled rage. I made a run for the flat and shut myself inside, grabbing a knife from the kitchen, crouching in terror behind the door as he shouted, swore, stomped and pounded outside. I felt very relieved when it finally died down. I don't know if he got bored, tired or distracted but at some point, he just walked away.

The incident and its effects died down after a short while. Then, a month or two later, I received a call at three in the morning from a police officer in Milton Keynes, a town just to the north of London. The officer told me that Darel had been picked up in a car park there, wandering around, talking to himself and generally acting suspiciously. He asked if Darel had any history of mental disturbance. I explained that he didn't but was probably on something and needed to sleep it off.

Was I not alarmed enough to seek help or walk away from the relationship? Why didn't I? Well, when you've decided to commit yourself to someone, you will find every reason to believe the best about them and push every sign of the worst aside. Besides, most of the time, he was himself, he was present. When he was, he could sometimes be cold, cruel and aggressive. Then, at other times, he could be loving and fun to be with. Besides, he never hit me and I was grateful for that, it could have been worse. Despite all the warnings, I clung to those good moments, the ones that seemed to prove my wish that everything would be okay.

By the time we were married, much to Darel's chagrin, I had formed a close-knit circle of friends that included Nigel and two new additions, Rachel and Reeni. They were my partners in crime for a good night out when Darel was off doing door duty at some or other nightclub, or making drug deals with his friends. He wasn't terribly pleased with my independence and later he would find ways to try to clamp it down.

With his drug dealing and my increasing social independence, not to mention the fact that most of our assets were in my name and I was paying the bills, tensions started to increase and we fought more often. I didn't realise that domestic tension was a sign of a dysfunctional marriage. As far as my experience had taught me, it was normal. My parents and Steve had shown me that fighting was just what couples did. It started to weigh on me, however, together with Darel's bizarre behaviour. Although I had gone through a long happy spell, I started to feel the familiar despair creeping up on me. My delinquent thoughts started to wander to ideas of suicide again – that old, cold comfort that assured me I could end it whenever I chose.

Perhaps it was my friends we were fighting about – the details of these arguments are never important in hindsight. When he was in a certain state of mind, he didn't need much provocation. The effects of drugs had us both on emotional rollercoasters and whatever may have started the fight, it soon escalated into disproportionate declarations of anger, resentment and mutual disdain. I didn't recognise it at the time, but I had been through this pattern before, almost word for word. My desperation to be heard, taken notice of, respected, rose to a fever pitch until finally I blurted out:

"I might as well just kill myself!"

Far from having the desired effect, this hysterical exclamation brought a smile to Darel's face.

"You haven't got the guts."

"Don't test me. I've tried it before and this time I'll get it right."

In that emotional state, we can never be truly conscious of the patterns and cyclical behaviours we are constantly expressing and perpetuating. You would think I couldn't miss the echoes of my mother's voice in my shrill threats of self-harm, or see the ghosts of her and Steve's gloating, goading expressions in his face. But at the time, obviously, that was the furthest thing from my conscious mind.

He actually laughed. "Well, go on then. Let's see you try."

And so it all played out again. I swallowed whatever pills I could find, sure that I couldn't fall short this time. I honestly thought it had worked as I lay down and felt consciousness slowly slipping away. So this was it then. What had I expected? Was there actually a moment there when I thought he might rush to stop me, declaring his love and appreciation for me, offering comfort and support, demanding that I never even think of self-harm again? I must have had some hope, no matter how remote. That was gone now, as all my vital functions slowed down and that terminal drowsiness crept over me. I welcomed it. I was now twenty-four years old; what was the point of carrying on?

What was the point of having been born in the first place? It was all so pathetic: a constant struggle, a few moments of hope that never seemed to lead anywhere – just tantalising dreams of things I would never have. My mother had been right, it seemed, nobody would ever love me – not in the way that other women are loved.

I woke up in hospital with my stomach being pumped and Darel nowhere in sight. I couldn't believe I had failed again. I went from feeling terrible for having failed a second attempt, to feeling even worse for having tried. Darel never even came to see me in hospital and when I was discharged, I simply went home and carried on. As a child, I had become used to unpleasant topics being carefully avoided and pushed aside. It was the way my parents handled anything too uncomfortable to discuss. Darel and I carried on this wonderful tradition; neither of us even mentioned the incident again.

By now thoroughly adept at burying trauma and slipping on masks with a conviction worthy of an Academy Award winner, I simply flowed back into life without a moment's thought. The day after my discharge from the hospital, I was back at work, dressed and made up, a smile on my face, in perfect professional mode.

Darel and I hadn't really bothered to reconcile – we just acted as if nothing had happened. That's what we did after every fight. Our married life simply flowed on and the first year went by as the years do. However, my obsession with marking milestones would not allow me to let our first anniversary just slip by. I was always conscious of the reason I had wanted to get married in the first place – I wanted a family. A year was long enough to wait and so, on that very day, I stopped taking the pill. Within a month, before I'd even taken any tests, I knew I was pregnant.

WENDY RICHARDS

Exciting, spontaneous, adventurous, loving, organised, dynamic, skilful, intelligent, caring, vivacious.

These are just a fraction of the words I would use to describe my friend, Wendy.

Last year I came to realise that we have so few opportunities in life to really express what we think and feel about our friends. So today, I would like to take this opportunity to let you know what I think about you, my friend, Wendy.

Now, don't get me wrong, I am not making you out to be a saint but you certainly have qualities that I constantly learn from.

One of these qualities I adore so much about you, is that you can set your mind to something and just simply do it. If we dwell too much on what could go wrong, we never seem to get around to do what we want to do and here you are today, having completed so much. Even when something does not turn out right, you use your abilities to fix it. I really doubt you will ever say "I wish I had done…" as you always seem to get on and do it.

Your skills as a mother and friend are outstanding. You have learnt this from no-one and you continue to be loving and supportive in every way. You are constantly learning and developing yourself and I can see you doing that forever more.

I personally have learnt so much from you and whenever I get stuck in a situation, I now reflect on what Wendy would do and then things always seem to sort themselves out.

So, Wendy, I could go on for hours, but I won't. I really just want you to know how much you mean to me and what an inspiration you are. Who would have ever thought all those years ago I would be saying that? But it's true.

Wendy, I love you so much, and you really mean the world to me. So carry on what you do as you do it so well, and I will keep learning from you.

Love to you always.
Your friend, Nige.
2006

CHAPTER SEVEN: MR BUMP

There was little to no chance of reconciling with my mother. I wasn't even sure if there was anything there to reconcile with; she would never be who I needed her to be. The truth was that I never really had a mother – not the kind that I had seen other children have when I was growing up. As I grew older, that empty void didn't get any easier to deal with. No matter what else occupied my thoughts, there was always this feeling of lack. It was like a constant pain in my heart, a throbbing reminder of how unloved I was. I was always asking myself why. Was I really that unlovable?

There was nobody who could act as a substitute either. I adored my paternal grandmother but she had passed on by the time I was married to Darel. I was on good terms with my mother-in-law, once the ice had been broken and the initial misunderstandings swept aside, but we weren't exactly close – there was still a distance there. There were no older women in my life that I could look to for examples of maternal love and strong femininity. Even as a child, I was determined to one day be the mother I never had. I made a promise to myself and my future children that I would be the best mother in the world.

In March 2000, barely a month after I had come off birth control, I knew my chance had come. How did I know? Well, I'm not sure if there is such a thing as a premonition or intuitive knowledge. I've stumbled unknowingly into too many unpleasant or ridiculous situations in my life for me to have any belief in the existence of some kind of inner voice, warning or heralding what lies ahead. If there is such a thing, however, I suppose this was it. It was a certainty I had felt only once before – the first time I had fallen pregnant when I was twelve. I didn't need any tests – I just knew. I felt it – and not in some airy-fairy sort of way. It was physical. I felt it in my body in the same way we feel pain or pleasure, good health or illness. The changes my body was then undergoing were subtle, but their presence did not escape my notice.

Just to confirm what I was already certain of, I took a home pregnancy test and I wasn't surprised when it showed up positive. A visit to the GP brought further confirmation. Later, Darel and I went to meet his parents at the airport as they arrived back from a trip to

Jamaica, and I held up a sign announcing that they were about to have another grandchild. Everyone was thrilled that a new member was about to be added to the Richards family. Everyone except Darel.

Not that he was unhappy about it – not at all. He just didn't seem particularly fazed one way or another. I was filled with excitement and nervous expectation. I was also terribly conscious of my inexperience. Was I even going to be competent for motherhood? What if I finally took the role only to find that I was no better at it than my mother was? It was Darel's fifth time as a father, however, and he didn't see it as a big deal. This awakened feelings of both resentment and fear. I resented the fact that he couldn't be as excited about our child as I was because he already had four others – and I was fearful that he was going to turn out to be a better parent than I hoped to be, or that I might meet with his disapproval if I wasn't a good mother. Darel always had a way of awakening these feelings of inferiority in me. When I was first getting to know him, for example, he had pointed out my poor dress sense, which was in marked contrast to the fastidious and extremely fashion-conscious attention he paid to his appearance. He just always seemed to have more experience, more knowledge, and this extended to the area of family.

Had I been older and wiser, I would have been able to see that this was far from the case. I should have realised at the time that appearance was all Darel had. Just because he had children already, that didn't make him a capable father. He gave the impression of a strong and competent adult man – few other men would want to engage him in a fight, and he had a way of wheeling, dealing and charming to get what he wanted. Yet he was unemployed, apart from the odd door duty at the clubs, he had no ambitions or prospects, had a drug habit, was living in a house that was in my name, driving a car that I had bought, depending on rental income from properties that I was managing. The internal clash between my fading first impressions of him and the revelations of the truth regarding his character led to a kind of cognitive dissonance. The image of the suave, charming and capable man who had walked into Tasty Bites that night, did not match the reality of the weak, addicted, unstable and narcissistic man-child with whom I now lived.

In addition, the more I learned about him, the more I started to feel a sense of pity or responsibility. I could have left him, as I sometimes thought of doing, but then where would he go? He was dysfunctional and increasingly not in his right mind. He was my husband and also now the father of my child. Surely, I couldn't just walk away?

The moment I knew I was pregnant, I stopped the drugs. I knew instinctively and with complete finality that this feature of my life, which had been so prevalent for years, was finished. The chapter was closed and a new one was about to begin. There was no withdrawal, no sense that I had lost anything – it was just over – and I have never looked back. Darel, on the other hand, was partying harder than ever though and there was no chance that he would give up his cocktail of cocaine and pills, which he needed on an almost daily basis now. I was quickly disillusioned of any hopes I might have had of him changing his ways on account of my pregnancy.

My twenty-fifth birthday came about two months after the announcement. Darel and I decided to take a weekend break in Newquay to celebrate. He must have been hoping for a repeat of our wedding, because one night, in a jovial mood, he presented me with several lines of coke. He was disappointed when I refused.

"Come on. Don't make me do it on my own."

"I'm not making you do anything."

"It's your birthday week. Let's celebrate like we always do."

"I'm pregnant, Darel." It was stating the obvious but I don't know – perhaps he did need reminding.

"All the more reason to celebrate then." He really was on another planet.

"No. I've told you before."

His demeanour changed to petulant anger very quickly. "Aw, you're like a wet blanket. Why do you have to be so boring?" Well, he said words to that effect anyway; in reality, there would have been several expletives peppered throughout his speech.

I stood my ground.

"Fine, I suppose I'll just have to celebrate on my own then." That was the most sense I got out of him for the rest of the holiday.

Even then, though, I still harboured some faith in the possibility that there was something I could do to get him to clean up his act. Maybe a permanent change of scenery would do the trick. This thought would lead to a life-changing decision a few years down the line.

Since Darel wasn't particularly keen on sharing in my excitement, I looked to my friends – Nigel in particular – to help me prepare. Over the years, our relationship had blossomed from being just colleagues to a friendship so close we became family. At times, Nigel seemed even more excited than I was and he would show this with frequent kind gestures. One day, for example, I arrived at my desk to find that he had left a card there, addressed to "Mr Bump."

"I just wanted to let your mummy read this to you so that you will know how wonderful she is," it read. "She is very much loved by everyone she comes into contact with. She has a beaming smile and sparkling eyes and you really can't help but love her... Your daddy is a very lucky man. We can't wait for you to arrive so you can see for yourself. I'm sure you won't be giving her too much hassle!. See you soon. Love Nigel." A kind, simple, off-hand gesture from a friend. It probably wouldn't prompt much more than a smile and a hug in people used to that kind of thing. But of course, I wasn't used to it. Cards, words of affirmation and tokens of love and affection were not common in my life. Standing there at my desk, I re-read the message a couple of times and then started sobbing. I immediately picked up my phone and called Nigel's extension.

When he answered, I could barely talk. He heard me crying and said, "I'm on my way." I can only imagine what he was thinking when he arrived at my desk and found that he had to comfort this emotional mother-to-be as she fell to pieces over a little card.

I finally pulled myself together and the over-the-top emotion of the moment passed, but the name, Mr Bump, stuck. Darel and I were still haggling over names so, from that day on, we all referred to the little person growing inside me as Mr Bump. Whatever his name was going to be, he was nearly here, and my life would never be the same. His arrival and my on-going life with him would prove to be the most important source of positive change I have ever encountered.

I still have that card, which I keep with many similar mementos. Because I lacked things like this in my earlier life, I have always tended to be very sentimental about them. I have held onto cards, letters, newspaper clippings, photographs that other people may easily forget about.

As my pregnancy progressed, I was painfully conscious of my lack of experience and knowledge. I was clueless – not that this makes me unique among first-time mothers but I felt as though everyone was more competent than I was. I had nobody to turn to for advice. Even if I were in contact with my mother, I did not regard her as a person I should go to for advice on mothering. Darel obviously couldn't offer much wisdom from the mother's side of the situation and what little support he could offer from a father's perspective, he was either unable or not particularly willing to give. He was too caught up in his partying and dodgy deals to show much interest anyway.

Thankfully, I was blessed with an easy pregnancy. I carried very small, a fact which, combined with my choice of maternity wear – fashionable, flattering and barely maternity wear at all – meant that many people didn't even notice my condition. I carried on with work and life as normal right up until the birth. So many of the major events of my life up to that point – and still to follow – were full of drama. It's remarkable how this most important of events was so peaceful. At times I thought it was too good to be true – was it supposed to be this easy? Wasn't there supposed to be discomfort and anxiety involved? There was constant reassurance all around me though, from friends and colleagues who were already mothers, from my veteran GP, and from Nigel, Rachel and Reeni.

I decided that a change in living space was called for. I felt it wasn't right to live in our little flat anymore – it was just too small. I wanted a house, where we could be a proper family. So I decided to buy a house and we moved in about five weeks before my due date. I even invested in new furniture and I was so paranoid about my waters breaking that I even kept the plastic covers on everything.

Only the week before Mr Bump emerged, I was busily organising the company's Christmas function. By this time, I was about four weeks away from the predicted day of arrival. It had been more than eight months without a single hitch, but I started to get very concerned about every little twinge, pain, change in the baby's position or any shift in my body's patterns. Many a time I believed I had cause to wonder if my waters had broken. More experienced women I knew assured me that when it happened, I would know all about it – there would be no room for doubt.

That Friday I came home from work as usual, preparing for what I thought would be an ordinary weekend. Now the discomfort was starting to set in, Mr Bump had moved to an awkward position towards my left side, and my back was killing me. I took a slow walk to my GP's office where he assured me that all was fine, although the old doctor did note that there was a chance I probably wouldn't make it through the entire three weeks. He couldn't give any indication of just how early the birth might happen though. I came home and sat down on the front steps of my house. Darel had gone out, where I didn't know, and I was alone. My lower back throbbed relentlessly and Mr. Bump, whom I had barely felt up to this point, was making me feel heavy and bloated, like some load I desperately wanted to put down. In that moment, the full enormity of everything came crashing down on me. Who was I to have a child? How was I going to handle this? What if I ended up having to raise Mr Bump on my own? I burst into tears, crying for the sad certainties of my life behind me and the scary uncertainties ahead.

The next day came and went as Saturdays normally did and Sunday seemed sure to do the same. I set about preparing the traditional roast that I usually made for us. It was a Jamaican variation on the familiar English Sunday lunch: roast chicken with rice and kidney beans. I nonchalantly popped the chicken in the oven, doing my best to ignore the aches that were creeping up my spine. They were getting hard to ignore though, so eventually I decided to phone the hospital. I would rather be safe than sorry, I thought. The nurse who answered the phone told me it was probably nothing but I should come in and get a check-up just in case. Darel drove me to the hospital, both of us expecting to be back in a short while.

This was not going to be as quick as I thought, however. The nurses knew there was no emergency because I had walked in and didn't seem to be in any real distress. They sat me down to wait for what ended up being about half an hour. Then I was ushered into the consulting room, my backache now becoming unbearable. Eventually, a nurse casually strolled in and did what I assumed were the usual checks.

"Oh…," she said.

"What?" I asked, ready to leap into panic mode at the slightest provocation.

"You're almost fully dilated. Baby's coming soon."

Was she joking? How was it even possible? My bloody waters,

which had been on my mind for the past month or more, hadn't even broken yet!

"He can't be."

"He certainly is. We'd better get you to a delivery room."

This was really it. I had chosen not to have an epidural but as the pains now intensified, I quickly changed my mind. They wouldn't give me one, however – it was too late for that. Instead they gave me a good dose of pethidine, which reminded me of many a wild weekend I had had before I fell pregnant. I went through the various contractions until I was told to push. The overwhelming physicality of the moment drove everything else out of my head but there was a brief instant, just before my child was fully out of me and the sound of his first cries filled my ears, that one random thought did pass through my mind: "Oh shit – I left the chicken in the oven!"

Mr. Bump had been born with slight jaundice, so he was taken away for examination immediately after the birth. We would spend the next week in hospital as a result of his condition. The nurses then brought me a telephone so that I could phone my family. I had no desire to call any of my actual family so I immediately dialled Nigel's number which, I was quite surprised to find, I knew by heart, even under the influence of the medication. My announcement to him was typical of the jovial banter that marked a lot of our interaction.

"Guess what?" I said once he had answered.

"What?"

"I've just had the baby."

"What? I'll be there as soon as I can."

"No, only joking."

"Don't do that!"

"Sorry, couldn't resist. Anyway, what are you up to?"

"Not much. Why? Do you feel like doing something?"

"Yeah."

"Well, what?"

"For starters, you'd better get to the hospital."

"Why? What's going on?"

"The thing is… I lied. I really have had the baby!"

After calling me a few choice names, Nigel made his way to my bedside in no time at all.

The boy formerly known as Mr Bump was swaddled and placed in my arms. As I laid eyes on him for the first time, I thought my heart would explode. My son – so strange to say or even think the words: my son. Here he was – and I was a mother, his mother. There is so much that has been said about the natural bond between mother and child that it's almost a cliché, but any woman who has actually felt it knows there is nothing passé about it. Besides, my experience shows that it's not a given: I don't think my mother, for instance, felt that for me, at my birth or at any time. If she had, I have no doubt my life would have turned out very differently. Reflecting on that now, I recall my mother telling me that Dad had only started to beat her after she fell pregnant with me. Perhaps that trauma had broken any bond my mother and I might have had, even before I had left the womb. I knew that nothing I had ever experienced could interfere with the love I felt for my son from the moment of his birth. Perhaps all my traumas had only helped to ensure that the bond would be stronger.

You can put that instant bond down to a surge of oxytocin, as the scientists do, or consider it something deeper than mere biochemistry. Either way, for me it was love at first sight – one of the closest things I've ever had to a spiritual experience. In that moment, with those as yet unfocused eyes looking up at me, I think I knew true love for the first time in my life. Real, unlimited, unconditional love. All my ideas of being the mother I never had, paled in significance compared to what I was now feeling. No thought could encapsulate it, no words could fully express it.

As I held my son in my arms, laughing and crying simultaneously, I thought to myself, "Well, you're here, my boy. So what's next?" He looked back at me, silent apart from the usual baby noises, mouth twisting slightly into what I imagined could be a smile, although it was surely only some involuntary nervous twitch.

"Well I don't know, Mum," I could picture him answering, "but whatever it is, I'm up for it if you are."

That imagined conversation fairly summed up the nature of our relationship to come. Almost nineteen years later, it still does.

*

Mr. Bump was still nameless at his birth and would remain so
for the next week. Darel and I had gone back and forth on the
possibilities for months and then had finally settled on Xavier. That
seemed set to be the one until I told a friend of mine, who then
pronounced it the Spanish way – "hah-vee-AIR". Not that I have
anything against Spanish names but after hearing that, it just didn't
sound right anymore. So we went back to the drawing board and came
up with nothing. By the time I unexpectedly found myself giving birth
on that December day, we still had not decided. When we drove away
from the hospital a week later on Christmas Eve, with our baby boy in
his car seat, Mr Bump was still the only name he had been given.

As I sat in the backseat next to my baby, on the way to to do
some last-minute Christmas shopping, I became keenly aware how
ridiculous it was that my child was still nameless. I had a book on
baby names with me, which a friend had given me, and I opened
it on a random page, as I sat in my car in the parking lot of my
local Sainsbury's supermarket. I found myself looking at the end
of the "T" section among the boy's names. I scanned the list until,
right near the bottom, my eyes came to rest on the name Tyreece.
I said it out loud a few times and it sounded good. Darel agreed –
surprisingly, since we seemed to agree on very little. So it was that
Mr Bump finally got his name.

Darel was with me throughout the delivery but it was not a

beautiful experience for him at all. He later described in gory detail how it disgusted him to watch me giving birth and how sexually off-putting it was. I should have known then that I was going to be on my own in my experience of parenthood.

My sense of incompetence when it came to the demands of motherhood was as strong as ever. I refused to even change nappies at first. In the hospital, the nurses handled it and once we brought him home, Darel took on the job, which he had done many times before. From the beginning, Darel was obsessed with our boy's appearance – I wasn't cleaning him right, dressing him right, doing his hair properly. Even as a baby, he needed to be dressed in designer clothes and if I chose to dress him in a cheap outfit from ASDA, then I was being a bad mother. Darel had always been obsessed with his own appearance and he now extended this to his son.

The first three years of Tyreece's life formed a slow but very fulfilling process of stepping into my role as a mother and strengthening the bond that was already so well developed at the time of his birth.

Although Darel was home during the day most of the time, he was never in a position to take care of Tyreece because he tended to sleep well into the afternoon and would always complain that we were making too much noise. So Ty and I soon discovered new adventures all around us. We would go to the airfield nearby and watch the planes coming and going, or to a farm in the vicinity to play with the ponies, donkeys, bunnies and goats. We would keep busy until about three in the afternoon, when I estimated Darel would be waking up, and then headed back home.

While Darel was projecting his extreme fashion consciousness onto Ty, I was making sure that he picked up my love of travel from a very early age. He was merely six weeks old when we took him away on his first European holiday – a trip to Luxembourg. The following year, we went to Venice. Within his first four years, Ty had travelled to six different countries.

These were precious moments and I knew that we would not have them forever. Before I knew it, the anxiously awaited Mr Bump was three-year-old Tyreece. In a blink of an eye, he would be twenty-something and going his own way. I was not going to let that time pass without fully enjoying it. Mostly, it was just the two of us. Even when Darel was there, he really wasn't. Day by day and year by year, Ty and I grew closer and closer.

As I was caught up in the growing joy of motherhood, my love for my son, as well as the demands of work, my childhood vision of life in a sunny paradise was never far from my mind. Yet, even though I had harboured the dream of travelling somewhere distant and settling there, I never knew how soon it would come true. As Tyreece and I sat at the airfield, watching planes rise up and shoot off towards their destinations, I was as unwitting as he was that we would soon be boarding a much bigger plane ourselves, setting off on another of our adventures towards a place we had not yet imagined. This would not be any mere holiday either. Where we were going would end up being home for the next two decades.

AN ODE TO WOOS

To our dear friend Wendy Woo
We want to say how much we'll miss you!
A true friend you have always been,
You've brightened our lives like a bright sunbeam
This may sound sappy and a little gay,
But before you go, some things we must say.
When you leave for the foreign land,
Our lives will seem somewhat bland.
You've made us laugh throughout the years,
With your crazy imagination and funny ideas.
Birthday outings & surprises galore
Of circus days out and sooo much more!
Memories of dancing and drinking Red Bull,
Cocktails, fancy dress & even paint ball!
Your drive & motivation for making things manifest,
Your generosity of clothes, we are the best dressed!
You've had the houses big and small,
But you're gonna make the best one of all!
With your lovely family and new beginnings,
To work hard as always to make your millions!
You deserve your dreams, you really do…
We'll miss you, OUR Wendy Woo!!!!!!

With love, Reeni & Rachel
2003

CHAPTER EIGHT: AFRICA CALLS

The plane descended among wild greenery, with rolling hills on one side and, on the other, the vast expanse of the Indian Ocean, receding gradually from sight as the plane neared the runway. A few minutes later, as I stepped off the plane, the warm balmy air, heavy with the scent of the sea, seemed to embrace me like an old friend. It felt like a homecoming, even though, only a short while back, I had to look up this destination on a map.

Darel, Ty and I were in the city of Durban, on South Africa's east coast. I didn't know exactly what would unfold there but I had a strong sense that this would provide the setting for our lives for the foreseeable future. I knew it before I had even learned anything about the city and the country. The feeling I had as we made our way through the airport, with the quick glimpses I caught of the surrounding landscape through the windows, reminded me of the dream destination I had visualised since I was a child. It wasn't that the appearance of Durban completely matched my fantasies. The specifics weren't the same but the feeling was. Even as we left the airport and hit the motorway, through urban steel and cement as I might have seen anywhere in the world, as far removed as one could get from any vision of tropical paradise, the feeling was undiminished. By the time I hit the beaches in suburbs like Amanzimtoti and Umhlanga, or spent a night in one of the nearly pristine wildernesses not far outside of the city limits, the feeling had grown to a certainty.

What were we doing here, nearly 10 000km away from our home in Brighton? At the time, we weren't exactly sure. We had told everyone we were here on holiday but that was not true. Darel and I had decided to make a permanent move some time before. When a friend of his, who was living in Durban, put out the invitation, we decided that this was going to be the place, even before I had looked the place up and interrogated a South African colleague of mine on some of the basics. There was certainly no plan in place. Neither of us left with any specific business or job prospects in mind. We both had our reasons for wanting the change of scenery and none of them really took long-term strategy into consideration.

For my part, I always knew the time would come when I would jet off to some warm destination far from home, so I didn't need much convincing. There was more to it though: I honestly hoped and believed that getting Darel out of the UK, away from our established way of life, would put the drugs out of his reach and prompt him to clean up his act. I foolishly believed that drugs wouldn't be a problem in South Africa! From his side, he had an assault charge pending against him after a coke-fueled brawl.

This must have made a fresh start, half a world away, a very attractive proposition for him.

Our numerous properties would provide us with the means for a good start. We decided to sell them all and use the cash as a down payment on what lay ahead. Although we had no definite plan, we had got a tip from Darel's connection that there were numerous housing developments underway in and around Durban. We would have the opportunity to buy units off plan and then resell them once they were completed. In the meantime, we could allow our investments to gestate. Durban had all we needed for a good life: a modern city with beautiful homes, fantastic beaches, all the trappings and a wealth of activities to keep us busy. There were good schools for Ty and we had every reason to believe that new business opportunities would arise. We would have the best weather in the world and the lowest cost of living in any South African city. We could travel to the surrounding countries, as well as South Africa's other major cities and tourist sites. The pros outweighed any cons, of which there really weren't any at that time, aside from having to leave home and friends behind.

After the initial three-week exploration, the decision was confirmed. We would head back only long enough to pack everything up in the UK and then return to Durban indefinitely.

I recall that, when I told Nigel, he smiled and assured me he would visit me, no matter where in the world I lived. I didn't realise it at the time but our friendship was about to get even stronger as a result of the distance between us.

The night before we were due to leave, Darel went out on a particularly epic bender and then passed out at dawn. Needless to say, as it neared time to leave for the airport, he was still asleep. I made the decision there and then that if he didn't wake up I was going without him. I phoned Nigel and told him that I would need a lift to the airport, with or without Darel. In the end though, Darel did wake up – and then a mad rush ensued.

When we first arrived in Durban, we lived an almost aristocratic existence. We couldn't get jobs because we didn't have work visas – not that this would have been in Darel's plans anyway. Luckily, the proceeds from our UK properties, together with the favorable exchange rate, afforded us a good lifestyle. Darel being as obsessed as he was with appearances, insisted that we find a ridiculously ostentatious place to live – far more extravagant than we could afford back home. So, we ended up renting a mansion in the upmarket suburb of Umhlanga Ridge, to the north of the city, a place for the rich. The appearance of wealth was rather thin, however. We could afford to rent the Umhlanga house but it was barely even furnished. It looked very grand on the exterior, but inside it was empty and lonely. We had first moved into a modest, three-bedroom place, now we were living in a six-bedroom house, with east and west wings, every room en suite, complete with a guest cottage.

Looking back, I can see it was a reckless move but it wasn't possible to reason with Darel. He believed that the bigger the house we had, the happier we would be. I was soon to discover just how unhappy I would be in this home.

*

How long would Darel actually stay clean for? It was naïve of me to think that drugs would not be an issue, just because we were in another country. I can't remember how long he went without but it wasn't long. One day he came home from the gym and told me in excited tones that he had met a new connection who would be able to set him up with both steroids and cocaine. My heart sank.

He was soon back to the routine that he had established in Brighton: stay up all night, taking drugs, collapse at dawn and sleep until three in the afternoon – then start all over again. The main difference now was that I was not at work anymore and so I would be at home with him the entire time. As I had done on the afternoons in Brighton, I made plans to take Ty out every day. Thankfully, there were so many options. We were once again near to an airfield and would spend hours watching planes and helicopters come and go. We also had our pick of animal farms and reserves nearby if we wanted to get into nature. Then there were the amazing beaches, and the water park. We were spoiled for choice and still caught up in the novelty of living in a new country.

Sometimes I would stand in one of the upstairs rooms of our oversized home and look out at the ocean view, ships on the horizon making their way southwards towards the harbor and overhead, the brightest blue sky I had ever seen. I was a long way from Brighton, let alone rural Wales. It was quite amazing when I stopped to think about it – the sequence of events that had resulted in me ending up here, on the opposite of the world, staring at this view – in Africa of all places.

South Africa is a country unlike any other – so very foreign to us in many ways and yet with just enough familiarity not to trigger a total culture shock. We could drive and walk down suburban streets like those we would have found in any Western country and had no need to learn a foreign language. Yet, a short drive in any direction would put us in the wilds of Africa. I loved it and still do. I was delighted to be able to indulge my love of animals here. Within months, we got a dog, and I was delighted with the troops of vervet monkeys that are known to live in and around Durban's suburbs, often passing through houses and gardens, pilfering food as they go.

*

Perhaps you may have been wondering what contact I had with

my mother over all those years since I left her to go into foster care. The answer is that there had not been much contact at all. We saw each other once when I was seventeen, without much meaningful interaction. I simply got on with a life that excluded her, suppressing my feelings of hurt into a deep, hollow void. A few months after Darel and I moved to South Africa, I begin to think a lot about her. I wondered if perhaps she had experienced any change of heart over the years. Maybe, I thought, we could finally talk things through. She may even be prepared to apologise for all she had allowed to happen. I fantasised about this reconciliation many times and I also wanted Ty to have a grandmother. So one day, I sat down and wrote an email to my mother. I wasn't expecting a response but I just wanted to extend an olive branch, whether or not it would be accepted. I didn't really say anything deep or provocative, I simply made an open offer to host her should she ever want to come to South Africa. I was quite shocked when the reply came the next day, saying that she would come in a few weeks!

I was apprehensive about seeing her again but I thought this was a good sign and happily began to prepare for her arrival. She had never flown before and I wanted to cut out the various travel complications as best I could. At the time, there were no direct flights from London to Durban. That meant she would have to change planes at Johannesburg. I decided to cut out that extra step and save her any additional anxiety by driving the 560km (348 mile) trip to pick her up instead. From the moment I met her at OR Tambo Airport, I began to suspect that I probably wouldn't get what I needed from this. I had set my expectations too high. I imagined some kind of tearful reunion, an acceptance, an apology. I might have known that wouldn't come but surely I had a right to expect something? She acted as if there had been no bad blood at all, no abuse, no rift. Cheerful and talkative, she went on about the basic details of air travel and luggage labelling, her dogs, standard tourist observations and so on.

I made a point of ensuring she had a good trip, setting up all kinds of activities I thought she would enjoy and sent her home without digging any deeper. She started to visit annually from then on and I continued to hope for a breakthrough. It took me years to accept that none would ever be forthcoming. As far as my desire to have her as a grandmother for Ty was concerned, that came to a pretty definitive end when I went out one day and left him in her care. By this time, Ty was old enough to express himself and he said to me when I got back: "Please don't leave me alone with Nanny Shirley – she's creepy." After taking her to the airport after that trip, I decided I couldn't passively wait for her to make some kind of overture towards true reconciliation.

I wrote her a lengthy email that night, laying everything out. I confronted her with the truth of the matter – that she was responsible for everything that had happened with Steve and that I needed her to acknowledge it and apologise. I received absolutely no response. She never contacted me again and I never tried to initiate contact either. I felt betrayed all over again. It was as if she had pulled a dagger out of my back only to thrust it in again.

The final episode in my relationship with her happened remotely. I discovered that my brother's wife had heard a very different story about me. My mother had told her that all the disaster that had befallen the family was my fault, that I was some sort of prodigal daughter, with loose morals and no respect for her parents. She was shocked when I finally sat down with her on a visit to England, and told her the whole story. She later confronted my mother with this and the woman who gave birth to me responded with the words that would serve as the death knell for any relationship we had ever had or might have. "I wish I'd never had her," she said, as my sister-in-law stared at her in shock. "As far as I'm concerned, she got everything she deserved."

In life, it seems, there are not always neat endings. Stories and conflicts don't always get resolved to our satisfaction. This is the case with my mother. Her hatred for me remains a mystery. My attempts to reconcile with her have been aborted and will never be taken up again. It took several attempts hosting her in South Africa and my son's sharp instincts about people for me to finally realise this.

Had it not been for my move to South Africa and the opportunities the new location offered to reach out to my mother, I may never have attempted to re-establish contact with her, and I would then never have been able to finally lay that ghost to rest.

*

It would not be long before I would realise that I'd had enough of life with Darel. South Africa was working out very well for me and Ty, but it didn't seem to be doing Darel any good. His bizarre behavior was getting worse and his aggressive and criminal episodes were becoming more frequent. I was oblivious to South Africa's racial politics but Darel was affected by it to some degree. His ego was so fragile and his concern about his appearance so hypersensitive that the slightest hint of insult, even if only perceived, would drive him crazy. Although he came from an entirely black family, he had a very light complexion, which prompted both white and black South Africans to refer to him as "coloured," a term used to mean, "mixed race." This was never said with any malice but it would always set off an argument, often with people as innocuous as petrol attendants or one of the many parking guards that are an ever-present feature across the country.

The odd habits he had picked up back home continued once we had settled in Durban. He was still talking to himself and I discovered that he had developed some more very strange habits, such as eating my make-up sponges! Well, what can I say about that? I have no words! It's strange to me now to think that I didn't say or do very much about all this at the time. It really was very bizarre, but it was the least of my trouble. It was his treatment of me and Ty that I was really worried about. When we were on our way to one of our first social events after having settled in the country, he turned to me and said, "You'd best let me do the talking because you really don't have anything interesting to say anyway." That was an indication of the way he thought of me – just sit and look pretty. He also started to set restrictions on my movements. I was only allowed to walk the dog within the confines of the walled estate we were living in at the time, and I was permitted to go out for breakfast with my new friend, Joanne. That was all. Other than that, I was not to go out on my own under any circumstances. Whenever we went out to a restaurant, I had to sit with my back to the rest of the diners so that no other man would catch my eye. One day, I found that he had gone out and shut me and Ty in the house. Every door was locked and no spare keys were left for me. This was no mistake on his part.

It seemed that his only concern for Ty was to make sure that he was always dressed properly and his hair done. He was like an accessory and anything I did to dress him was wrong. One of the main events that pushed me towards the life-changing decision I was about to make started off with a simple father-son event at Ty's school. Ty and the other boys in his class were meant to come to school with their fathers, with whom they would then team up on a craft activity. Of course, when the time came for them to head to the school, Darel was fast asleep. I struggled to wake him and when I eventually did, he took his usual hour to get ready, picking his outfit, doing his hair, making sure everything was perfect. We were so late that, by the time we got to school, the other kids were already coming out of the class with their fathers, proudly carrying the fruit of their labour. My heart broke for Ty as I looked at him and saw the tears rolling down his cheeks. It wasn't the final straw but it was very close.

After that, I gave Darel an ultimatum: he had to choose whether he wanted the drugs or Ty and me. He told me blatantly that it wasn't a fair choice. At that point my mind was made up about the future of my relationship but, as had been the case with my schoolfriend having to push me to tell the teacher about Steve's abuse, it would take something more to spur me into action.

All of the hurts and dramas accumulated until the decisive event came in the form of a holiday to Swaziland. Swaziland is a tiny country wedged between South Africa and Mozambique, and we had heard it was beautiful. We decided to take a road trip there for what I hoped would be a memorable family holiday. And memorable it certainly was!

The trip from Durban to the Swazi border takes about five hours, mostly on a long stretch of the N2 highway. We were not far from the border post, with probably about another half an hour of travel before we would pass through. Darel was driving and he was in a particularly jumpy and aggressive mood. I would have driven but he insisted, adding some dismissive comment about my driving skills. As the long road stretched on, I looked over my shoulder at Tyreece – he was dozing in the backseat. I watched the landscape fly by through the passenger window, enjoying the hilly greenery, imagining this new piece of Africa that I was about to see. Darel was speeding along in the right-hand lane of the two-lane highway. Up ahead of us I could see two big trucks, one behind the other, in the left-hand lane. We would have just whizzed straight past them, except that the driver of the rear truck decided to swing into our lane to overtake the other one. It was far enough ahead of us for Darel to slow down in time and then it would take only a few seconds before the truck went back into its lane and we could continue straight and pick up speed again.

Darel completely overreacted, as if he had been cut off or driven off the road. Going into a rage, he accelerated so that he was driving right up against the truck's rear, pressing the hooter as he went. Once the truck had passed the other one, it moved over to the left, leaving the road clear for us to pass. That should have been the end of it, but Darel wasn't finished. As we passed the cab, he leaned over me and glared, shouting obscenities, at the truck driver, who looked down at us with a puzzled expression. Then Darel moved over into the left-hand lane and slowed the car to a crawl in front of the truck. When it tried to get around us, he would move over to block the way. He gestured for the driver to pull over, which he eventually did, presumably because he saw he wasn't going to get anywhere until this situation was resolved. Darel pulled over in front of him. By this time, I was frantic, shouting at Darel to leave it alone, but he wasn't even hearing me. He threw open his door and got out of the car, marching over to the truck. Ty and I turned to watch through the back window.

The truck driver climbed down from his cab and Darel barely gave him time to put his feet on the ground. He was a much older and smaller man than Darel and didn't stand a chance. There was a lot of shouting and pushing. It seemed that this would be the fullest extent of the fight when Darel turned back towards the car. From my position in the passenger seat, looking back through the rear windscreen, I could see Darel walking towards us and behind him, the driver reaching up into his cab. My first thought was that he was going to get a gun. I told Ty to lie down between the seats and then shouted at Darel to get into the car so we could get out of there straight away. That only made him turn back to look at the truck driver, who was now facing towards him again, not with a gun, but with a heavy steel pole. Darel lunged at him and a short struggle ensued. Even armed, the old man was no match for Darel, who managed to get the pole off him and then proceeded to beat him furiously. The man collapsed under the blows, his screams drowned by my own as I shouted at Darel to stop. The trucker ultimately fell silent and Darel threw the pole away and got back in the car. He started it up and calmly drove off. Through the back window, I could see the old truck driver lying motionless on the ground. I had no idea if he was alive or not – I still don't. I felt terrible and my mind was full of questions: would he be alright? What about his family? Further along the highway, police cars and emergency vehicles raced past us in the opposite direction, heading towards the scene.

We stopped at the border post and got out of the car. It was then that I saw that the rear of the car was splashed with blood. It seemed that nobody else had noticed. We could not be easier to spot now: a black man and a white woman with a young boy, travelling in a blood-splattered car.

We continued across the border and went to our resort. However, there was no way we could just have a pleasant family holiday now. Darel tried to be sweet and make it up to me but it was too late. At my insistence, we headed home early.

One evening, back at home, as I tucked Ty into bed, he asked me a question that really got me thinking. "Mum, was Dad the baddie that day on the road?"

I had been toying with the idea of a major change for some time now. As I sat wondering how to answer Ty's question and remembered looking down at the back of our car splashed with an innocent man's blood, I made up my mind. When was I going to learn? How long did I have to let bad situations carry on before I put a stop to them?

*

About a month later, we were back in the UK on a visit. Darel had a court appearance to get to and I desperately needed to see a friendly face. I called Nigel at work and told him I needed to see him. He met me on his lunch break on the Palace Pier in Brighton. I broke down at the sight of him, years' worth of pent up pain and stress exploding from me. He hugged me tight, not asking what was wrong. I think he knew and he was waiting for me to get it out.

"I'm leaving him," I said finally.

I had no clue how I was going to get Darel to give me a divorce or how I would deal with the backlash. As fate would have it, no big plan was necessary. We were booked into The Grand, one of Brighton's fanciest hotels – Darel keeping up appearances again. As we sat in our overpriced room one day, something sparked a fight. The actual content of the argument is a blur to me now – it really doesn't matter. The point is that the words came out of Darel's mouth with no prompting from me, although he did not anticipate my response:

"Well we might as well get divorced then!" he shouted.

I didn't stop and think about my answer. It was out of my mouth before I even knew it:

"Yes, we might as well because I can't do this anymore."

There was a moment of silence as he stared blankly at me, slowly computing what I just said.

"Fine, we will then."

I went into the bathroom and locked myself in, fearing that some angry reprisal might follow once the reality had hit home. Sure enough, a few minutes later, he came knocking on the door.

"Wendy, open up," I heard him say on the other side of the door, all the anger gone from his voice.

"I just need to be alone now, Darel," I answered.

He knocked harder and the edge of anger came back into his voice. "You're still my wife. Open this door or I will break it down."

He started to pound on the door and violently rattle the handle, spouting a torrent of barely coherent abuse. I don't know how long he carried on like that but at some point, he just stopped, as he had done years before after I had turned us back from that drive to London. In his fragile mental state, he tended not to focus on any one thing for very long. As abruptly as he had begun, he stopped, the room went silent and then I heard the door open and close.

*

The flight back to South Africa would have been an extremely awkward one if we were on it together. Thankfully, Ty and I flew back first, leaving Darel to attend his court hearing. He was due to follow back to South Africa a week or two later. Several months before, we had left the Umhlanga mansion. I knew it was unsustainable and unrealistic and finally got Darel to move to a smaller home in the inland suburb of Hillcrest. It was there that Ty and I now headed, packing up all of our belongings and promptly moving to a flat I found for us. Darel was absolutely furious when he came back to find us gone. I had underestimated his narcissistic rage and so I was not prepared for the coming backlash.

CHAPTER NINE: THE LADDER BREAKS

Is there anything she can't handle? She's been broken. She's been knocked down. She's been defeated. She's felt pain that most couldn't handle. She looks fear in the face year after year, day after day, but yet she never runs. She never hides and she always finds a way to get back up. She is unbreakable. She is a warrior. She's Me.

Darel's backlash started immediately, although it would take some time to build up to its fullest, ugliest heights. I had not really thought any further than getting myself and Ty out of the house. With that done, my focus was on finalising the divorce and I trusted that everything would be better after that. I suspect that Darel, however, had already devised his revenge plan, though I do wonder if he knew beforehand how easy it would be for him to carry it out. That amazes me to this day.

From his point of view, I had done a serious injury to his pride and ego by daring to cut ties with him, and I needed to be punished for that. The retaliation started with comparatively small things – although they didn't seem small at the time. Although I had left the house, I still offered to continue doing his laundry for him, like the conditioned abuse victim I was. I would go around when I dropped or picked up Ty and collect his dirty laundry. What was I thinking? I just knew that nobody else would do it for him. He was more alone in South Africa than I was and I suppose I felt sorry for him.

This routine went on for a few weeks without incident. He mostly maintained an angry silence when we were in the same room – which didn't happen often or for very long periods of time. This changed one day, however, when I discovered that he had taken the first step in his "revenge." I dropped off his laundry and was on my way out the door when he stopped me.

"Come have a look at this," he said, with a smirk and a satisfied glint in his eye.

I was immediately on the defence. What could he possibly want to show me? He took me over to the fancy dining room table he had insisted we buy. It was high quality and ornate and was long enough to seat far more people than we had ever entertained during the time we lived in that house. There was a white tablecloth draped over it, but other than that, it was completely bare.

"What?" I asked with a mix of impatience and confusion.

He looked at me with that mysterious, smug smile, then reached out and whipped the cloth off the table. My heart sank.

Spread out on the shiny surface of the table were several photographs – all of me. I hadn't seen these pictures for a very long time – in fact, I had almost forgotten about them. Only once had Darel ever convinced me to pose nude for him. It was many years before when I was only eighteen. It hadn't really occurred to me that he would keep the photos, or that he would ever have a use for them, but here they were. He had printed them out and added speech bubbles to them, filled with various mean-spirited profanities. It was obvious what he intended to do even before he announced it: "I'm going to send these to everyone in your address book." Yes, he had access to my address book, because that was another thing I hadn't thought of when I left.

I was mortified and already feeling the potential humiliation. My mind quickly scanned through some of the names in my address book. Oh God: my friends, old co-workers, my friends' parents, distant family members, Ty's schoolteachers! I should add that, had I ever known that these photos would see the light of day and be looked at by anyone other than him, I might have at least put more effort into them! They featured me posing shyly and half-heartedly, pulling back the top half of a bathrobe to reveal my breasts – this in a variety of positions and settings. They would have been embarrassing even if they weren't so tentative and amateurish.

I tried to make light of it so he wouldn't see how rattled I was. He even had his laptop at the ready with the address book onscreen so he could gloat each time I cringed over a particular name. He was determined to be thorough: for those people who didn't have email addresses, he planned to print the pictures and post them. I kept my poker face on and then burst out laughing when he pointed out my grandmother's name. "She passed away two months ago," I said.

He carried on behaving as if he was very pleased with himself though. I wonder how much time he had spent on that exercise – thinking about it, printing the pictures, writing up the speech bubbles. I knew he had a lot of time on his hands but this was ridiculous. I left the house still pretending to laugh it all off. However, when I got home, I feverishly set about contacting everyone I knew to warn them of the mails they may soon receive. Everyone responded in good humour and after a few days of anxiety, I finally relaxed in the knowledge that any crisis this situation may present was averted. It really was a laughable situation in the end – the only damage done would have been to my self-image and that had taken worse blows. I didn't hear anything from anyone on my mailing list and so I thought that perhaps Darel had decided not to follow through on his threat. I discovered decades later, however, to my horror, that he had actually sent them. Everybody had just been discreet about it to save me the embarrassment.

I hoped that this childish stunt would represent the limit of his attempts to hurt me and tarnish my reputation. I think I knew though, that I had not seen anywhere near the worst he could do. This was barely a taste of the revenge he had in store.

*

One of the worst things about that unhappy period was that my relationship with Ty started to suffer. During his visits with Darel, his head would be filled with all kinds of ideas about what a bad mother I was. I can only imagine the half of what was said. When he came home, I could feel that he was different with me – colder, more distant, uncooperative, with occasional outbursts loaded with the things he had picked up from Darel: I didn't dress him properly so I didn't love him – and similar things. It was deeply hurtful, not because any of the things that he was saying were true – they weren't – but because he was succeeding in poisoning our son against me, or so it seemed. He clearly had more influence on Ty than I had thought, but this is understandable considering that Ty was only three at the time. Ty wasn't the only person who was susceptible to Darel, however. If I didn't know it before, I would find out soon enough: Darel had a way of getting people to think and do what he wanted them to.

This state of affairs went on for a few weeks, with tensions simmering but seldom boiling over. There would be the odd confrontation which would usually end in a slew of insults, but that was about it. There were no further attempts for a while, that I knew of, to do serious damage. I don't know if he was lying in wait until the right moment or if he took his next step on an impulse. Either one was entirely possible with him.

*

I stared at the words on the ATM screen: "Insufficient funds." As I felt that familiar sinking feeling that I had known, ever since I had decided to divorce Darel, could never be too far away, I pushed it aside with the thought that it must be a mistake. The accounts were in Darel's name and he could just withdraw everything if he wanted to. I had naively thought that he wouldn't since much of that money was really mine. A fifty/fifty split on the divorce was a legal necessity but was really quite generous from my point of view, since most of that money had been made from my efforts.

In the absence of the funds in those accounts, there was only one other way I could access money to live on. A firm of conveyancing attorneys were holding deposits that we had made on our off-plan property purchases. I would need to get that money back now. Speaking to the lawyer who dealt with our affairs, I couldn't help but pick up on the icy disapproval that came through her friendly professionalism. He had been here, I thought, and must have spun her quite a tale. I explained the situation to her and she frowned at me.

"But, Mrs Richards, the funds were transferred out of the account yesterday. You authorised the transaction."

I stared in disbelief.

"I certainly did not."

She sounded alarmed now. "But... you phoned."

I shook my head, unable to talk, unable to believe what was

happening, unable to work out how it was possible.

"I thought it was you," she said. "It was a woman with a British accent."

"Are you telling me you authorised the transfer of all the funds on the basis of a phonecall?"

Apparently someone pretending to be me had called in and explained that she ('I') was gravely ill – too sick to go into the attorneys' offices. The planned transactions on the properties were to be cancelled and the remaining funds were to be transferred into a particular account, which Darel had nominated. This would have to happen without 'me' being present but Darel would come into the office with the necessary signed documents. He then went along and finished the transaction, having forged my signature, complete with sob stories about his 'sick wife'. Evidently, the performance was very convincing. He walked out of those offices having transferred every single cent into a UK account. I have never been able to confirm who the woman with the British accent was but I have my suspicions.

Once again, just like when I first moved to Swansea when I was sixteen, I had nothing – not even a bit of change to buy a loaf of bread. This was worse, however, far worse. Now I was no longer alone. How was I going to feed my child? The day after the meeting with the attorneys was Ty's fourth birthday party. I now couldn't afford to pay for anything. A friend of mine paid for the food but, as the jumping castle I had ordered was being set up, I stared at it with a knot forming in my stomach. I didn't have the heart to disappoint Ty by telling them to take it away. I made some excuse about not having the money at the time but committed to make payment the next day.

I was now desperate. I didn't even have money for groceries, let alone rent. I did something I had not tried doing for a very long time: I called my dad. We had been in touch over the years. He did wish me happy birthday some years but forgot most of the time. I was forced to do something I had sworn, years ago in Swansea, that I would never do – I had to ask him for money. His reply was not surprising but nonetheless devastating: "If you must insist on living an unrealistic lifestyle in a country halfway around the world, then you'll have to do it on your own." As I ended the call, I silently scolded myself for doing what I promised I would never do. I renewed that vow to myself there and then, but with an important modification: not only would I never call on my father for help again, I would make sure that the need to do so would never again arise. It didn't feel like a very powerful resolution in that moment as I sat wiping tears from my eyes, wondering how I was going to support us.

Ultimately it was Nigel who came to my rescue, sending me enough money to get the immediate necessities. All the people who helped me out had faith that I was good for it, despite my current situation. I knew it too, or kept reassuring myself of the fact, although it was hard for me to believe at the time. I certainly had no idea how I was going to get myself out of this. It's always difficult, in those moments of extreme testing in our lives, to see a way out. I didn't see one then but I held onto the stubborn belief that it would come somehow. I was positive, I was determined, I would make a plan.

Of course, Darel was unreachable. He wouldn't answer the phone and he was not at home when I tried going there. He had gone into hiding and I had no doubt that he was planning to leave the country, if he hadn't already done so. The attorneys opened a case of fraud at the Durban North police station and a warrant was put out for his arrest. I doubted very much that he would ever allow himself to be caught. Although he was keeping a very low profile, I asked the neighbour, Sam to keep an eye out for him and let me and the police know when Darel came home. One day, Sam called me to say that Darel was back. He had peeked over the wall to see my soon-to-be ex-husband busily packing boxes. Within an hour or two, a convoy of police officers arrived at the house I used to share with him and arrested him. He denied all charges but surrendered his passport, as he was pending trial, and was released on bail. I knew then and there that he would find his way out of the country. Confiscating his passport meant nothing; he would get another one as soon as he was able. This was Darel we were dealing with, and no-one told Darel what to do – not even the police.

Then a scary thought occurred to me: there was a strong possibility that the final act in his revenge would be to get his hands on Ty. That would be the final, devastating blow. I alerted both the police and Ty's school to this possibility. A few days later, I received the call from the school to say that Darel had indeed been there to try to pick Ty up, saying that he had arranged it with me. The staff refused to let Ty go and called the police. Darel promptly made himself scarce again.

Later that same day, the police called to advise me that Darel had been stopped at O.R. Tambo International Airport in Johannesburg. As if in a scene from some action film, police officers went onto the airliner after he had already boarded to arrest him, escorting him off in handcuffs in front of a planeload of confused passengers. He was then loaded into the back of a police van and driven all the way back to Durban for his date with the magistrate.

After his arrest, his luggage had been taken off the flight and left with unclaimed baggage at the airport. I called the airline and asked them if I could collect it. I was taking a chance and was sure they wouldn't let me, but I just told them I was his wife, concerned about my husband's luggage, and they agreed without any further questions. I wanted to see what he had in that bag. He was fleeing the country and I wanted to know what he planned to take with him. I could probably have found no truer reflection of his state of mind than the contents of that suitcase. There weren't many items of clothing but there were several pairs of new, expensive, name-brand training shoes, a few pairs of damp underwear – representing another of his odd predilections, bathing in his underpants; "I like the way it feels," he told me once – and his collection of porn magazines. Returning to the house, I found several photographs of Ty strewn across the lounge floor. He had packed a random selection of things but, in his haste, hadn't even bothered to take any pictures of his son. I repacked his bag with only the left of each of pair of shoes and with his porn collection displayed on the top so that it would be the first thing anyone would see if they needed to open and inspect it. It was a petty thing to do, I know, but no less so than his photo stunt, and it was probably the most satisfaction I was likely to get out of this conflict.

Darel pleaded guilty in exchange for a non-custodial sentence and agreed to be deported. Had his legal advisors not gone for that option, he would have been heading to Westville Prison, a jail on the western edge of Durban, which has notoriously held both violent criminals and high profile participants in the South African government's various corruption scandals. The money he took was never returned. A short while later, he flew back to the UK and out of my and Ty's lives, never to speak to either of us again. He never checked on us, he never contributed to Ty's maintenance in any way, he never even called or sent a card on any of Ty's birthdays. He has never made a single call or sent a single email to see how his son has managed any of the events in his young life. He left me to fend for myself and Ty on my own. That betrayal and abandonment was hard to take – even from him – but in the long run, it has been a blessing, for both me and Ty. On returning to the UK, however, Darel evidently related a very different version of events to mutual friends and even to my father. He has always been a master of manipulating the truth.

I had no idea what the future would hold now. I was a single mother in a foreign country with not a solitary pound, rand, penny or cent to my name. I had no car, no food, and no means of paying rent. I was unemployed and had no business or investment prospects. However, a life-changing new development was already taking shape. Before the dust had even settled, there was another man in my life. My relationship with Darel had been the cause of a lot of pain; this new entanglement was set to bring a very different kind of heartache.

A lot of people – people who have been blessed with families and upbringings that they might describe as "normal," often take their ordinary lives for granted. Some even disparage their lives, wishing for something more interesting. Well, as someone whose life has certainly been "interesting," all I've ever wanted was normality. As a child, I looked at some of my friends, who lived in stable homes with two loving parents, and I wished I could have what they had. All my life, from my childhood to Ty's birth and beyond, I wanted to have that, I wanted the home and family I had never had. With Darel I knew this was impossible from very early on but I carried on with him anyway. In fact I accepted that loving, comfortable normality was something I would probably just never be able to get. I would create as much as of it as possible for Ty but the romantic ideal was not for a girl like me. That was just the way it was.

And then there was Tristam.

CHAPTER TEN: FLYING HIGH

Sometimes the bad things that happen in our lives put us directly on the path to the best things that will ever happen to us.

By the time my divorce was underway, with all its drama, Tristam had actually been a presence in my life for some time. Some months before that final explosion in the hotel in Brighton, I had booked something special for Darel's birthday. This was part of a tradition I had started for myself and my closest family and friends. I would celebrate birthdays by setting up what became known as "poop-your-pants" experiences, organising some new, boundary-pushing activity each year. The intent is always to keep the adventure a complete secret right up until the last minute, building excitement and trepidation. This time I planned to take Darel for a paragliding flight over the KwaZulu-Natal Midlands, a short distance inland of Durban, near the Drakensberg Mountains.

The day finally came and we arrived at the airfield, me brimming with excitement and Darel characteristically underwhelmed. I didn't know it at the time but this was soon to be a moment of definition. My life was about to change in a way I could never have anticipated. That pivotal second happened instantly when the pilot came out to greet us. Amidst the introductions and pleasantries, something I could not define seemed to be clicking into place. This rugged and self-confident man, several years older than me, in great shape and with a head of greying hair that made him look wise and distinguished – a "silver fox" if ever there was one – immediately caught my eye. This was an amazing and rather uneasy experience for me, because no man had caught my eye since Darel had walked into Tasty Bites that night over a decade before. I was so conditioned, after years of Darel's obsessive jealousy, not to look at any other men. If they showed interest in me, I either pointedly ignored them or was completely oblivious. I didn't even talk to other men, unless it was absolutely necessary, for fear of Darel accusing me of infidelity, which he would do at the slightest provocation. So, for me to take notice of another man, to engage in that butterfly-inducing first eye contact and feel that surge of attraction, was an impossibly rare thing. It was a feeling I hadn't felt before. The pilot had an easy-going attitude but was also very self-assured. There was great strength under his gentle approach, which I found very appealing. That was Tristam.

The attraction was immediate and – as I later discovered, mutual – but neither of us did anything about it then. Tristam took Darel up on his flight as arranged, and Darel came back looking bored. My flight, on the other hand, quite literally changed my life. This was how I found myself flying above that incredible, mountainous landscape, feeling like I was in free flight, as if my childhood dreams of seeing the world from a bird's eye-view were coming true. It was an epiphany, a fulfilment of an almost forgotten dream. I turned my gaze from the landscape in front of me to the pilot behind me – the smiling stranger who somehow didn't seem a stranger to me at all. I was overwhelmed by feelings of love and freedom I had only fantasised about, as close to a sense of destiny as I had ever felt in my life.

In the days and weeks that followed, I often found my thoughts wandering to Tristam. What could this mean? Had I met someone special? Could this be true love? "Love at first flight?" Was there even such a thing? After my return from the UK trip that finally ended my marriage, I sat down and wrote Tristam an e-mail, expressing what I felt in my heart. It was an ardent and romantic expression, yet also so very innocent. It felt like a renewal; it was a return to a red-cheeked, schoolgirl innocence that I had never before been able to experience. On the one hand, it was very much an open and honest declaration from one adult to another, but on the other, it evoked the feeling of a love note secretly passed from desk to desk while the teacher wasn't looking. I had been robbed of those experiences of young, unaffected love but this gave me an opportunity to gain some sense of how it might have felt – one of many things I can thank Tristam for.

We became a couple instantly. Our relationship moved with incredible speed as love ignited. Tris was the opposite of Darel in every respect. He was what South Africans would recognise as a real KwaZulu-Natal boy: he was unpretentious, lived a simple life, had a love for the great outdoors, was happiest either on the beach or camping in the bush and could usually be found walking around without shoes. Added to this was his love of flying, which was a driving passion for him and which he had turned into his livelihood. Like most white South African men around his age, he had done compulsory service in the old South African Defence Force, where he had served as a paratrooper. A divorcee with two children, he also had sound family values and quickly showed unexpected paternal love for Ty. He was always calm, always the voice of reason, and always "the man with a plan". All of this was in stark contrast to Darel's lack of motivation, obsession with keeping up appearances, total disregard for family, and self-centred hedonism. I fell in love with Tris because he was everything I didn't have and had always wanted. Was this the love I had always dreamed of? Surely I deserved to be loved. Was I finally getting what I deserved?

I was financially destitute by the time I fell in love with Tris, but he was able to show me how much joy could be drawn out of life without the need for money. He also provided the inspiration for the business venture that would get me on my feet again. On one of our early dates, at a Thai restaurant in Hillcrest, I wondered aloud how I was going to make money to sustain Ty and myself. He suggested that I join his paragliding business and manage sales. I immediately thought much bigger and took that idea several steps further, as it dawned on me that I could run a good business facilitating aviation activities of all kinds: paragliding, skydiving, helicopter flights, hot air balloons, and more. So instantly, Sky Adventures was born – a business to which I devoted my heart and soul for the next few years. It was a difficult path at first. Some months I would have to choose whether to spend the little money I had on Ty's school fees or on essential business expenses. However, I gradually established myself and developed a thriving business, which I later sold profitably as a going concern – an achievement of which I am very proud.

In keeping with the tradition I had long since set for establishing and measuring milestones in my life, Ty and I moved in with Tristam on my birthday. We had been together for just ten months by then, but it felt like the three of us were a perfect family, and Tris and I the perfect couple. It was almost too good to be true. Ty had a father figure and I finally had a dream partner. Little did I know how short-lived this blissful situation was to be.

One thing I found enormously gratifying was the way that Tris took Ty under his wing. Prominent among the memories of that time is a bookshelf that Tris built during the time we were settling in, with

Ty's help. I recall taking a photograph of the two of them proudly posing with it. The beaming, sparkling-eyed smile on Ty's face just seemed to sum up how we all felt about the situation.

About three weeks after we moved in, the novelty of the situation having not yet worn off, I was fully immersed in my work at Sky Adventures. It was really taking off – pun intended – at a very pleasing rate. It had been conceptualised from pure necessity to provide a means of support for Ty and myself. Yet, it quickly became a passion that now occupied most of my waking hours. Having a partner who was an experienced professional in the same industry made it all the more exciting. Even our holidays revolved around flying. The Christmas before we moved in together, we had taken a trip to the gorgeous, forest-nestled, coastal town of Knysna, where we camped for three weeks. Ty and I had never camped before and we loved this rustic adventure. We took to the sky almost every day there – Ty included. Just as I had fallen in love with Tris, I also fell in love with flying and the feeling of absolute freedom it brought. Seeing the world from above with the wind coursing over your body is a sight and an experience that not even the view from a plane window can prepare you for. Had my childhood dreams come true?

I decided that I was not content merely to facilitate flying or just to be a passenger – I wanted to fly myself and I was going to train to be a paragliding pilot in my own right. Tris and I purchased Sky Adventures' first paragliding wing and one chilly June morning, in that third week after we had moved in together, we took it out so that he could test it. I watched in excitement as he took off, knowing that soon I would be up there flying solo. I watched him launch himself into the air and glide as normal and then I stood helplessly as the wing collapsed and suddenly descended to the ground. I had no idea what had happened and for an agonising few minutes, the fear that something had gone terribly wrong paralysed me. Was he hurt – or worse? Thankfully, although the flight hadn't worked out, Tris was completely unharmed. He explained to me what had gone wrong – technical matters which I no longer remember. Those minutes between when he dropped and when I saw his face again were terrifying. We realised that it could have all ended right there and then. We both received the message loud and clear that nothing in life should ever be taken for granted, least of all the people we love.

Later that evening, as we discussed it, he showed me a printout of that very first email I had sent him ten months before, in which I had confessed my feelings for him. We marvelled at the fact that so many months had already passed. I looked at the flowers he had bought me earlier that week, as well as the card that had accompanied them. He had written how grateful he was that I had come into his life. How lucky could two people be? Ten months is really nothing in the grand scheme of things but so much had happened in that time. It had all developed so quickly and here we were, feeling like we had known and loved each other all our lives, and shaken up by the fact that it could have all been over in just a few seconds.

The next day, the sunrise brought a gorgeous morning that was absolutely perfect for flying. As a pilot, Tris's life revolved around the weather. Each day would start with a careful assessment of the day's conditions to decide whether any flights arranged for that day could go ahead or not. He was very pleased with what he saw when he looked out of the window that morning. It was Father's Day and a family had booked Tris to take their 70-year-old dad on a paratrike flight over the area around Nagle Dam near Pietermaritzburg. This is a stunning stretch of land, which has its very own Table Mountain, not to be confused with its much more famous namesake on the other side of the country in Cape Town. That day the air was cool, crisp and clear – the visibility would be outstanding. Tris's client was in for an incredible experience.

Ty was also very excited about Father's Day, as he now had someone he could celebrate with, a true father figure. Tristam got up early and started getting ready for his flight. As I lay awake in bed, I could hear him and Ty in the living room and I smiled to myself. With my help, Ty had prepared a Father's Day card for Tris. He had probably been waiting for some time for Tris to emerge from our bedroom so that he could give it to him. I heard Ty calling him, I heard Tris's warm expression of thanks, followed by a few seconds of muffled conversation. The comforting warmth I felt in my bed on that winter morning was no match for the glow I felt inside. This was what I had wanted all my life – it wasn't about external conditions, possessions or the house in which I lived. The sense of love and calm that embraced my entire being in that instant – that was the true home I had fantasised about. It was as if I had been holding my breath for years and now, finally, I could exhale.

Tris came through to the bedroom and kissed me goodbye, the card in his hand, still unopened. Then he went off to do his work, looking forward to the Father's Day celebrations Ty and I had planned for him.

What can I say about the next few hours? There is nothing to say, really. It was just a normal Sunday morning. How often do we allow minutes, hours, days, even years in our lives to pass in settled passivity, unconscious of the fact that our lives are changing before our very eyes? Yet another defining moment was sneaking up on me and I didn't suspect a thing. The phone rang and I thought nothing of it: just another phone call, they happen all the time. It took a moment to process what the voice on the end of the line was saying. How could such a thing happen? Why? What were the chances? There was no way this could even be a possibility. It was Father's Day and we had celebrations planned. Besides, we had only known each other ten months. I felt a cold shiver shoot up my spine, as I shook uncontrollably. I refused to believe this was true.

But it was.

The person who called me was a friend of Tris's – another pilot.

He explained that Tris and his client had taken off without problems that morning. Then, halfway into the flight, they had hit a power line. The cable snapped, sending hundreds of volts through Tris's body. Miraculously, he still managed to land the trike. Once it was safely on the ground, Tris had collapsed into his passenger's arms – and it was there that he died seconds later. When I went to collect Tris's van, I found Ty's Father's Day card in the cubbyhole, opened. Tris must have read it just before he went on his final flight. Holding that little token of love, that symbol of a family that now could never be, I cried uncontrollably. I cried for my loss, and for Ty's. How was I going to break this news to him? Only months after we had started rebuilding our lives, it was shattered. It was like thousands of jigsaw puzzle pieces, which had been so painstakingly put together, were now broken apart irreparably, the pretty picture they had formed dissolving into tiny fragments.

Just as I had done years before, I dug deep and found strength I never knew I had. I had to show Ty that everything would be okay. Although I was crying inside, I put on a brave smile and carried on. As I told a friend of mine one day when she asked me how I was coping, "this is terrible. I can't tell you how devastating this is. Yet the horrible truth is that I've been through worse."

That was how I lost the first man who really loved me. Perhaps there's truth in the saying that all good things must come to an end. Well this was a good thing – a very good thing – and now it had ended. Considering where I was when Tris entered my life, compared to where I was when he so suddenly left it, having imparted so much love, wisdom and healing in so short a time, it seems all too appropriate that he had wings.

WHY I LOVE YOU

Dear Mum
Thanks for teaching me the best things in life I love you so much! You're the best mom a boy could ever ask for.
Thanx 4 loving me 24/7
Thanx for the love u bring
Thanx 4 the happiness
Thanx for the memories
Thanx for always making time for me.
I love u because you make me laugh.
I love u because you make me happy.
I love u because u r sweet
I love u so much
I love u because u watch TV programmes with me.
U make me giggle and laugh. U r nice to me.
You are the best mom ever! Thanx for being an awesome mom and everything you have done for me.
-        Tyreece, aged 8

CHAPTER ELEVEN: THE FINAL BETRAYAL

"Don't get mad. Don't get even. Do better. Much better. Rise above. Become so engulfed in your own success that you forget it ever happened."
Donald Driver

A bubbly little number with spicy overtones, a classy, independent chick with a sense of humour and a zest for life, looking for a partner in crime to dine out with, train with and share adventures. So, gentlemen, if you're looking for a quickie, are a player, married or a smoker, please look elsewhere. If, however, you have an entrepreneurial mindset, are sporty, enjoy a healthy lifestyle, and entertaining conversation, let's chat.

This was me according to the dating website I signed up to about two years after Tris's death. I still think it describes me rather well and I had faith that it would attract the right kind of man.

Since that terrible Father's Day, my life as a businesswoman and as a mother had grown from strength to strength. I threw myself into both roles with more passion and determination than ever before. The independence I had developed in my teenage years stood me in excellent stead now as I carved out my own niche, even as I was still a single woman in a foreign country, supporting a child on my own. The work was hard but this kind of independence had come easy to me for many years. Yet, despite building and selling successful businesses on my own, despite balancing work and personal life with relative ease, despite being Ty's mum, dad and best friend all rolled into one, I still felt incomplete. I still hoped to find that perfect partner, that perfect father figure and role model for Ty, and form the family I continued to dream of, even in the wake of Darel's disaster and Tris's tragedy.

I had dated two men in the meantime. In fact, I had started casually seeing one of them only a few months after Tris's death. It was my way of dealing with the loss; I simply couldn't stand being alone. The second followed a few months later. Neither of them got anywhere near serious, neither of them was what I was looking for. I kept myself out there and continued to hope. I created the profile to aid in this search. After a number of respondents ranging from interesting to completely out of the question, one popped up that held my attention:

A sporty family man, recently separated, looking for a lady to talk, train and just generally have a good time with.

Not as creative or as long as mine, but then my experience had shown that men's profiles seldom were. He was quite attractive from what I could see in his pictures, and the 'family man' bit was certainly appealing. I responded to his initial contact and we started to exchange emails. For months, that's all we did. Every single day, I looked forward to reading his messages and writing my responses. These were no limited-character texts either; they were essays! We questioned and answered and joked, discussed our children and our plans. Yet, we never made plans to meet up. We never even exchanged phone numbers. I suppose that should have been a sign. We may never have met in person had I not made the first move.

I was hosting a glamourous business event at a hotel and was staying overnight. I invited him to come and see me while I was there. We had already said so much to each other through our emails, that I honestly felt like I knew him. The anticipation of finally getting to meet him face to face was intense. I was like a teenager with a crush, with all the excitement and anxiety that comes with the prospect of being in the company of this person I had built up and idealised. The feeling was intensified by the fact that he did not turn up at the time we had arranged. I sat in my room and waited… and waited. Two hours later, he finally called to say he had arrived downstairs. That should have been another sign right there – one of many that I missed.

We had dinner together and, putting aside his lateness, he was exactly what I hoped he would be. The conversation went from revisiting some of the things we had said in our messages to each other – there was a lot of ground to cover – to picking up on things that neither of us had yet thought to explore. It flowed naturally – we clicked, we laughed, we talked about our kids. It didn't feel like our first meeting at all because we had already told each other so much. He was as attractive and charming in person as I had imagined him to be.

His family situation immediately gave rise to some questions, however. He explained that he was living in the cottage on his property while his wife and children lived in the main house. He had not yet left or got divorced, he said, because he was staying for the children's sake. I overrode the doubts this raised in my mind, telling myself that this was a very mature way to handle the breakdown of his marriage. He was clearly a good father.

So began my six years with Clinton.

Like every other stage of my life, this new development soon formed a new routine. Clinton and I would see each other several times a week, he would stay over at my place, but he would always get up early and make sure that he was home before his children awoke. That went on for about a year. He continued to stay married and continued to stay on the same property as his wife, for two years – for the sake of his children, of course. After about six months, I began to wonder if he was ever going to take the next step.

One evening, we were due to go out and I called him to confirm the time. I was calling on his mobile phone, not a landline, so imagine my surprise when a woman answered. Slightly thrown, I asked to speak to Clinton.

"Who's speaking?"

"It's Wendy."

"Oh. Hi, Wendy. Just a moment, he's busy getting ready." That's how I spoke to Clinton's wife for the first time. It was perhaps one of the most surreal moments in my life. There I was speaking to my boyfriend's ex-wife – except she wasn't technically an ex. She evidently knew about me and appeared totally unaffected by the situation. I could not find it in me to be so comfortable with the strangeness of this arrangement, however. I didn't think I could let it go on much longer and I told him so.

"If you really want to stay with your wife, you need to tell me now and stop wasting my time," I said one evening as we sat on my couch after dinner. I would normally have had a glass of wine in my hand at this point but he had often expressed his distaste with me ever drinking alcohol. Ever eager to please, I never drank in front of him now.

"Stop worrying about that. It's over with her. I couldn't even be attracted to her again. She's not the same woman she was when we met. She's put on so much weight… I just couldn't."

I left a long pause after that delightful revelation. It would one day leave me bewildered when I met her years later and saw she was one of the most beautiful woman I had ever seen.

"I understood you still living there when we met, but it's been months now."

Looking back, his response was infuriating. He didn't get angry or defensive, he just placed his hand on my leg in a patronising way, a comforting half-smile on his face, a smile that said, "Leave it to me. I know better."

"I've told you," he said, "I have to stay for the kids."

"For how long?"

"Just until they're a bit older and they can deal with it."

I thought about Ty and how he had dealt with his single-parent life. His father hadn't given him time to deal with anything and he was turning out fine. This would be a stark contrast to Clinton's two children, who would still have both their parents and a stepmother.

"Listen, my angel," he said. He always called me 'angel'. To this day, I cannot stand being called that and cringe when I hear the word. "Just be patient with me and I promise you, we will live together and be a family, as soon as the time is right. Do you know what I'm going to do? This is another reason I've been staying – I've been saving on rent – because I've got a plan. One day, I'm going to build a house for you, me and Ty. My kids will come too of course. We'll be a real family. I promise you that but please, just wait a while. Be patient."

He reiterated that story to me time and time again, in slightly different forms, during the time we were together. It was so what I wanted to hear. He knew what I wanted and he hit the mark exactly.

How I wanted to believe it. For this beautiful dream, I was prepared to tolerate Clinton staying at his wife's home for a little while longer. After all, it was clear that it was me he loved. He spent most of his time with me, he trained with me, he ate with me, he slept with me. He told me he loved me every single day. He never did any of that with her. I could be patient. I had the strength to wait – and wait I would.

For three years, I was not allowed to meet Clinton's children. "It would be too confusing for them," he explained. He never really specified as to when it would no longer be confusing. Was I to wait until they were over twenty-one? Then, one day, something happened that should have made the truth of this situation all too clear. Ty and I went to a pet expo in Durban Central one Saturday, and lo and behold, as we turned and walked up a row of stalls, there was Clinton, coming the other way with his son and daughter. I raised my hand and was about to call out when he just walked on by, acting as if he hadn't seen us. This was impossible since we were barely a few feet away from each other. He just ignored us, pretended we weren't there. My phone pinged two minutes later with a rushed, explanatory text message: "Sorry, angel. It's just I've got the kids with me. But will see you later."

That was the moment it should have ended, isn't it? What more evidence would I have needed that this was not going anywhere good? Yet, I explained and justified everything away. It was a tricky situation after all, I reasoned. It would get sorted out.

Three years into our strange courtship, he finally made a move to placate me. He moved out of the cottage in his wife's garden to a room in his mother's house. He couldn't get a place of his own, he said, because he was still saving his money. Our family house wasn't going to pay for itself, after all. He would spend a night or two each week at my place. That soon became three nights and finally six nights per week. Every Sunday night, he would head off to his mother's place and sleep there, then he would be back on Monday. He was, by then, a resident in my house in all but name, and his stopping one day short of spending entire weeks with me meant that he was free of any financial obligations in my household. He was just a guest after all.

In the meantime, Ty and I would still have to put up with being non-existent as far as his family was concerned. As had so often happened in my life, some of the hardest revelations came over Christmas time. Since the first year, I had been begging to meet the children but he always brushed me off. On Christmas Day, he would go off and have the traditional dinner with his wife, children and other family members. Ty and I were not invited. I had hoped this would change after he had moved out of his marital home. The following December, he stayed with me on Christmas Eve and the next morning, he casually kissed me goodbye and went off to the usual family celebration at his mother's house, leaving me and Ty in our house alone.

I had been through so many lonely Christmases by this point that I should have been used to it. It was still something I couldn't stomach though, and why should I have to? I was no longer that solitary teenager in a bedsit in Swansea. I was a grown woman with a son and I had a man who was supposed to love me, with a family of his own that could have opened their arms to us. The bleakness of those Christmas Days are hard to express. I had always managed to make birthdays into joyous occasions regardless of the circumstances, but Christmas somehow always managed to get me down.

That day, Clinton had set off to his mother's house with gifts for his children – gifts which I had bought. I pride myself on being an excellent gift-giver and, to please him and score points with the family that didn't seem to want anything to do with me, I chose perfect presents for the children. "You can even say they're from you," I said. He considered it as if he was about to make some kind of grand concession to me and then nodded in agreement. So, off he went, with the presents I had chosen and paid for. Later he was generous enough to come back with photographs he had taken of the kids with their new treasures.

As Ty and I sat together at our own Christmas lunch, he looked at me and said, "His family just don't like us, that's all." He had only just turned twelve but he had a wisdom and directness that were well beyond his years, as he still does. It made me so sad, because this latest rejection from Clinton and his family was nothing new to him. This was how he had understood the world from a young age. There was me and him and there were close friends like Nigel and Claire, and the rest of the world would simply hurt and disappoint us if given the chance. It broke my heart.

That all seemed to change about three years after Clinton and I started dating. The living arrangements didn't change and neither did his official marital status. Nonetheless he, in his infinite wisdom and generosity, finally decided to reward my patience by allowing me to meet the children. I could not have anticipated how smitten I would be with them. His daughter was about two years younger than Ty and his son was another two years younger than that. They were friendly, open, fun, well-raised with excellent manners – just wonderful. Ty and I both took a liking to them and we formed a strong bond. I remember saying to them a number of times over the following years that there had to be something wrong with them – they were just too perfect! They loved me saying that, their bright eyes beamed with joy at the revelation of how perfect they were.

With that it seemed that we were actually one step closer to having a dream setup with a beautiful extended family. Sure, Clinton had not yet got divorced, started building that house, or even offered to contribute to my home in any proper way but he had finally allowed me to get to know his kids. We were moving in the right direction.

I made every effort to be an ideal stepmother and I was delighted to find that the kids appreciated me and reciprocated. The five of us would spend weekends together, we would have 'poop-your-pants' experiences together on birthdays, we would go on all kinds of outings and enjoy plenty of quality time together at my house, I even started teaching his daughter how to ride a horse. Another highlight was the rescue puppies that I started to foster.

I often thought back to the day my father had drowned those puppies. I never forgot their smell – that unmistakable puppy smell. It stayed with me forever. I couldn't change what had happened when I was a child, but I could certainly make a difference now. So I began my puppy fostering journey. Over the space of two years, I fostered a total of twenty-eight puppies. Each one arrived broken, just a few weeks old and in desperate need of love and care. Perhaps, in some strange way, they reminded me of myself once upon a time.

The kids loved the arrival of each new puppy, pouring love and affection on them as I went about rearing the tiny creatures to continue their lives in their 'forever homes.' One day, Adam and Eve arrived. Eve was a typical puppy: playful and adventurous. Her brother, on the other hand, was very different. He was lost, sickly timid and sad, needing extra care and love. Over the next few weeks of setting my alarm every three hours for feeding, we bonded. He was different to all the other pups. He behaved as if he truly believed I was his mum and wouldn't let me out of his sight. He was the one that stole my heart. Much to the kids' delight, we adopted him, naming him Rocky. Today he is healthy and strong and enjoys running with me through the bush. I remembered the lamb I had fostered when I was a teenager living at Dad's place in Wales. It was very soon after I moved there, the horrors of Aldershot still fresh in my mind. This one still had her tail, which she used to wriggle frantically as she sucked on the milk-filled Coke bottle, with the big rubber teat attached, which I used to feed her. She even slept in my bed and woke me when she was hungry.

*

The Christmas after I was finally introduced to Clinton's kids, Ty and I were invited to join the celebrations – after the formal dinner had been completed. The year after that, we finally received the nod to take part in the actual Christmas dinner. Surely now, I could see that Clinton was right? I just had to be patient. Things were going exactly where I wanted them to, it would just take time.

It was disappointing, however, that Clinton didn't reciprocate my efforts with his children by reaching out to Ty. Whereas I embraced his children almost as my own, he just tolerated my son, seeing him as a hindrance, someone he would have to put up with or get around in order to get to me. I remember one December, as I decorated the Christmas tree, I broke down in tears and begged him to make an effort if only for my sake. He offered words of comfort but never did as I asked. Looking back, Ty has often told me that he had never fully opened up to Clinton anyway. As he often tells me: "There was always something shady about Clinton."

Despite all the doubts I had, one thing I was assured of was Clinton's faithfulness to me. I had come to accept that he could be selfish and oblivious to others' needs. That was a fault of his – one that I learned to navigate quite effectively. After all, he could also be extremely affectionate and would lavish me with love and flattery.

He was also, so I thought, the complete opposite of Darel; he didn't touch drugs and wasn't even a drinker. These were important factors because of my years with Darel. Even with all of his shortcomings, he was a faithful man, and even if he might be inclined to stray, I thought, I would make absolutely sure he would never want to. He would be hard pressed to find a woman who ticked so many boxes. I kept in shape – in fact we trained together – I cooked and cleaned, I was not financially dependent on him, I was a committed and involved stepmother to his kids, plus I was willing and able to satisfy each and every one of his needs in the bedroom. He, like Darel, was a man with some disturbingly particular sexual habits. Given my sexual history, it's not surprising that I attracted two men with such tastes. Clinton was particularly voracious in his appetites. Darel's desires had often been dampened by the drugs he used but this was not the case with Clinton – I had to be able to perform every day, regardless of how tired I may be, regardless of what else was happening. Failure to do so would not bring any kind of angry eruption, it would just result in a lingering silent treatment, accompanied by boyish sulking, which I would have to dig through to find out what I had done wrong. He even got me to stop doing trail races on Sunday mornings – something I enjoyed very much – because Sunday morning was bedroom time.

He was also possessive, controlling and jealous. Early on in our relationship, he had expressed his dislike for a woman drinking alcohol. I only drank on the one night in the week when he was not at my house or when one of us was away. Not that I was a heavy drinker but I appreciated sitting back with a glass of wine or a gin and tonic after a long week. Aside from bedroom performance, there were certain other things that were expected of me on a regular basis. One year, Ty and I went off on a safari getaway with Nigel and Claire, another close friend who had entered my life a short while after Tris's death. Clinton opted to stay behind, saying he couldn't afford the trip. On the first night away I got a call from him.

"Why haven't you sent me any pictures today?" he whined, like a child who hadn't got the sweets he was promised.

"Are you joking?"

"You have to at least give me a sexy pic or two. How am I supposed to get by without my daily dose?"

"Clinton, I'm sharing a room with Ty. Surely you can wait a couple of days."

"Fine," he said before hanging up.

On another occasion, he went off to Cape Town to do the annual Argus cycle tour. He was a keen cyclist and this is probably the most important race on the South African cycling calendar. I couldn't go with him that year, so I took the time to catch up with my friends. In particular, I was looking forward to spending time with Claire. We had plans to go out to dinner and as we got into our Uber taxi, Clinton called.

"Hey, what are you doing?"

"Claire and I are just getting into an Uber. We…"

"What are you doing in an Uber?"

"Claire and I are going out."

"To drink, I suppose. Where are you going?"

"Just to…"

"What are you wearing?"

"Nothing fancy. Just jeans, a T-shirt. It's not a formal occasion or anything."

"Send me a picture. I want to see what you're wearing."

"What?"

"I'm away for just a few days and off you go, out on the town, going who knows where and meeting who knows who. I want to see what you're wearing."

I took a selfie and sent it, proving that I was casually dressed and wearing nothing revealing.

One morning, I took the children to school and came back to find him sitting in front of my laptop. He hadn't expected me back so soon and I caught him unawares. When I asked him what he was doing, he evidently decided not to go with some cover story. I probably hadn't given him enough time to think of one.

"I just wanted to check if you were hiding something."

"What would I be hiding? Why don't you just ask?"

"Like you'd tell me. I saw what you did earlier."

"What did I do?"

"I walked in and you quickly closed the Window you were working in. There was obviously something you didn't want me to see."

I tried to remember what I had been working on earlier that morning. It wasn't unusual for me to be flitting back and forth from one tab to another and switching between Windows.

"That's ridiculous. I was working."

I looked at my screen and saw there was a software installation in progress.

"What's that?"

He stood in sheepish silence before answering. "It's spyware," he said. His tune changed now. "I'm sorry, I needed to know. I just love you so much, it makes me crazy. You can't blame me for being jealous."

That was the story to account for his jealousy whenever it arose. He loved me so much, he didn't want to lose me, it was normal to be jealous. I kept my laptop away from him after that. If he could install spyware, what could he do with my information? I learned to take his jealousy with a pinch of salt, however. Darel had been the same. Maybe, I thought, this is just how men are? Maybe that's just how they show their love?

*

In the early days of our relationship, I had often raised the subject of more children. I really wanted to have at least one more. He always put off the discussion: "Yeah, let me think about it. We'll discuss it in six months." Six months later, he would give me the same response. As Ty and I were finally brought into the family fold, I began to reconsider. There was already a big enough family. I had Ty, Clinton had his two children, we were all getting on nicely, and perhaps there was no need to bring another child into the picture. I began to toy with the idea of having a tubal ligation.

I sat down with him and discussed it one day and he was very supportive. He agreed that it was probably for the best, sharing my thoughts on the size of the family and the number of children. He raised no protest, at no point did he ever mention that the future was unpredictable and I shouldn't shut that door. It was my decision but, considering what was to come, what was to be revealed, he might at least have discouraged me from taking such a drastic, final step. I went through with it in the end and he held my hand every step of the way, no doubt having calculated that this was entirely to his benefit.

Towards the end of our fourth year together, Clinton finally made a stunning confession. It had been such a good year and I admit, I was in a bit of a bubble. I had established a relationship with the kids, whom I adored. Ty was getting on well with them. Clinton and I were in a good place and we seemed to understand each other. Everything was looking up. It was strange how the subject came out of nowhere. I don't know why he chose to tell me then. Perhaps his conscience had been gnawing at him. As we lay in bed one night, he broke the comfortable silence to reveal that, during that first year when we were together, he had not been living in the garden cottage – he never had. He had still been sleeping with his wife. A year later, he had moved into a separate room inside the house, which is where he had stayed until he had moved to his mother's.

It was a punch in the stomach but I had had worse. It seemed to me though that Darel's financial betrayal had just been topped by this act of dishonesty, this further abuse of trust.

"And after that? You moved out of her room and never slept with her again?" I asked.

"Absolutely. I swear it."

"You also swore – on your children's lives – that you had long stopped sleeping with her. Why should I believe you now?"

"Do you know how much it's taken for me to tell you this? Why would I tell you and then hold anything back?"

"Is there anything else you need to tell me?"

"Nothing."

"Are you sure?"

"Nothing, angel, really. I swear to you, there is nothing else, and it's all over and there's nothing more to tell."

Well naturally, I ended it right there. I couldn't have that – a man who was having a sexual relationship with two women at the same time, while casually lying about it. I should have read the signs before anyway. This was the final straw. I told him to leave and never come back.

I wish that were true. What actually happened was that I accepted his apology and his promises and we carried on for another two years.

*

My relationship with Clinton had all started with an online conversation and that was the way it was destined to end. It happened one night after I had been working late. It was exactly a year after the Uber incident, and Clinton was off doing the Argus again. I had dropped him off at the airport that morning, kissed him goodbye, and handed him the good luck cards that the three kids had made for him. Neither of us guessed that this would be the last time we would see each other. That night I arrived home after a long day. Checking my phone, I saw that someone I didn't know had sent me a message on Facebook. It was a woman by the name of Sandra and what she said made me feel as though an icy knife had been driven into my heart. Yet another pivotal moment of painful definition was about to play out.

Hi Wendy. You don't know me but I need to tell you something about Clinton. I know he's away and I thought now would be a good time to reach out to you.

Clinton and I met about four years ago. He told me that he was separated from his wife but still staying in the same home with her for the children's sake. We started a relationship and I have been coming to South Africa to visit him regularly since then. I live in Germany. Recently I was trying to get him to take the relationship to the next level, but he wouldn't. I couldn't understand why he wouldn't divorce his wife. Imagine my shock when I discovered that he had already moved out of her house and had been in a relationship with you for six years. I threatened to tell you everything but he begged me not to for the children's sake. I'm sorry about this, but I thought you needed to know."

She attached several naked pictures of Clinton that he had sent to her – pictures he had taken while standing in my bedroom. She also sent pictures of them together at their regular meeting place, the Riverside Hotel in Durban North.

I was shaking, my blood was cold.

I phoned Claire in a state, barely able to express myself coherently. – I desperately needed support because I was feeling something welling up in me and I had no idea where it was coming from or where it would take me. Claire offered to come over but, since it was late, I told her not to worry. I then called Clinton.

"Howzit, angel," he answered.

"Clinton, is there anything you need to tell me?"

"No… Why do you ask?"

"Are you sure?"

"Yeah, absolutely. What's wrong, angel?"

"I just got an email from Sandra."

There was a moment's silence that seemed to last an eternity. I could almost hear the cogs in his head turning as he processed this information.

"Oh fuck," was all he had to say.

He barely gave me time to say anything else before he jumped into his next thought: "I'll get divorced! Then we can finally live together as a family like we always said we would."

I ended the call and I blocked him on WhatsApp. He tried to call my phone several times and when I didn't answer, he tried Ty's phone.

This was not just the end of my relationship with Clinton. There was something much deeper happening. It was as if some long dormant volcano was bubbling and boiling inside me. The truth was that it had been for years, for decades. Now finally, it was about to erupt. I didn't just feel this one new betrayal alone. It was as if every previous insult and injury were being dredged up from somewhere deep inside me. I saw Clinton's smiling face, glibly spewing assurances, expressions of love, compliments that I now knew were just empty flatteries. In my mind's eye, that face became Steve's, leering and gloating. Then it became Darel's, telling me dismissively that I had nothing to say, laughing at me as he encouraged me to kill myself. I saw Tris's lifeless body. I saw my father smashing my mother's head against a wall. I heard my mother telling me to "be a good girl." I imagined her telling my sister-in-law that I had got what I deserved. It all rushed through my mind and heart in a single instant. All of those memories, all of those emotions, came to the surface and exploded out of me in a burst of rage the likes of which I had never imagined I could feel, let alone express.

I was on and off the phone with Claire and Nigel. I don't even remember what I was saying. Claire later told me that she had never heard me talk like that before. For one thing she had never seen or heard me angry, never heard me say these things. Yet it wasn't so much what I was saying but the way I was saying them. When I was a child and we first moved from Trelech to Aldershot, I had been teased terribly for my Welsh accent. I had worked hard to root it out and had finally mastered the southern English speech of my schoolmates. After a few years, my Welsh accent was nothing but a memory. As I now raged, I lapsed unconsciously back into that Carmarthenshire lilt of my girlhood. It was as if I was someone else entirely! As if this last injury had pushed me over the edge into some sort of regression. Young Wendy, who had never been able to do anything but tolerate what was dished out to her, was now coming out to get her own back!

I ran around my house like a mad woman, pulling up every one of Clinton's possessions that I could find and destroying it in the most appropriate way possible. On my dressing table, I found the bottle of Angel perfume he had given me on my last birthday, and I smashed it. Nobody would ever call me angel again. I took the shards of the bottle and tipped them into his laptop bag, before taking out his computer – his livelihood as an IT professional – cracking the screen and then picking off every key with a knife. In between each of these little acts of retribution, I would take a picture of what I had done, unblock Clinton, send him the picture and then block him again. It was petty but it was all I could do at the time. It is probably just as well that Clinton was not there. In that state of mind, it is very likely that I might have got violent with him. I would not have been able to control myself. This was the final act of betrayal I would ever allow myself to face. I had put up with one after another – my mother, Steve, Darel and now Clinton, this man who claimed to love me. Every dismissive gesture, every unkind word, every hurt, every single rape that Steve had subjected me to – it all somehow culminated in this moment. I did not have the reflective capacity at the time to understand this – in fact I could barely think straight at all – but later I knew it to be the case.

Amidst my rampage, a thought occurred to me: why was I wasting time with all of these little things when Clinton's pride and joy was in my garage? The cherished collector's item he preened and fawned over as often as he could – a restored old Ford Cortina from God knows when. Steve had also been a vintage car lover, I remembered. I went into the garage and grabbed the heaviest hammer I could find. Swinging as hard as I could, I brought it down on the windscreen. Who knew it would be so hard to break a windscreen? The hammer bounced and I was thrown off balance, having swung with all my strength. I brought it down again and again and I can't describe the satisfaction I felt as the glass finally cracked and then shattered. I was reminded of that moment when my father had thrown a brick through the front window of the Trelech house, but this time, I was the one doing the breaking. I wasn't the passive, helpless child caught in the cascade of glass.

As night gave way to early morning I damaged or completely destroyed everything that Clinton had left in my house. He tried to contact me for a long time after that but I never spoke to him again.

It was done, I had cut him off and I would never let him back in, even for the most mundane of discussions. This was only the beginning of my recovery, however. The following day I had to drive Ty to school and behave like I was holding it all together. The moment I drove away, the thin veneer I had pasted up just cracked and crumbled. I shouldn't even have been behind the wheel of a car. My emotional state was such that I could barely remember how to get back home.

My next stop was at my bank. Remembering the day when I found Clinton installing spyware on my computer and then recalling what Darel did to me before he fled the country, I put two and two together and suddenly feared that Clinton might have a way to steal the small savings I had managed to accrue. I sat in front of the customer consultant with absolute composure, just as I had always managed to do – good, sensible Wendy just taking care of business, betraying no sign of the fact that the bottom of my world had dropped out. As I walked out of the bank, however, I lost control. Everything around me seemed to blur and converge into a senseless mess in which left, right, front, back, up and down no longer had any meaning. I stared at the parking lot as sobs racked my body. I couldn't even remember where I had parked my car. It took weeks, if not months, for me to pull myself back together into a semblance of genuine inner functionality to match the appearance of outward control I had constructed.

This episode drove home to me the importance of friendship. Without Claire and Nigel – who did what he could from a distance

– I have no idea how I would have coped. I had come apart in a spectacular way but thankfully there were at least two people who knew how to put me back together again. And then there was Ty – my reason for wanting to put myself back together in the first place. For years I had being trying to create the perfect family, little knowing that I already had it.

I still miss Clinton's children. I had grown to love them almost as if they were my own. I cut contact with the family on the very night I heard the news but I have been fortunate to remain in contact with the two children. We don't talk much but the lines are at least open to reach out in either direction. As time went by, I found out more about Clinton and his marriage and the part I had truly played in his life during those six years. I had thought I had found a true partner, a man I loved and wanted to spend my life with, and with whom I could have a family. It became apparent that I had initially been nothing but a "side piece" in a marriage, as was the other woman, Sandra. Clinton did eventually get divorced, almost immediately after I ended it with him, perhaps in an attempt to win me back. If that was the case, it is possible that he had, in his really confused way, developed some kind of true feelings for me. On the other hand, he probably just couldn't stand to lose such an abundant and compliant source of narcissistic supply.

On many occasions he accused me of being bipolar; it was his way of controlling my anxiety and mental state. The reality was that he had the problem, later confessing to being a sex addict and promising to seek therapy. Although he admitted to the addiction, he claimed that I was the one responsible for making him that way.

As the storm cleared and I gained distance and perspective on the matter, I remembered a message I received one night a few months before I discovered the truth. It came from a man who regularly cycled with Clinton. It said that he had seen him out and about with another woman. I had jumped to Clinton's defence, asking this stranger how he dared to accuse him. Clinton, who was in the bed beside me at the time, then accused me of having some secret admirer who was trying to break us up.

Later, Ty reminded me of one of Clinton's running jokes. He would frequently say to his son and to Ty, "It doesn't matter how many girlfriends you have, as long as you don't get caught," always followed by a wink and a chuckle. Except it was no joke – or rather, the joke was on him in the end. So many signs that I didn't see – or refused to see. How could I not have known that this man had lied to me. He had exploited me for six years, using me as a sex accessory in much the same way Steve had done. He had told me every day he loved me just as Steve had done too. I realised that I had never really known what love was, not romantic love anyway. I had the love of my son and my friends, but the love that a man and woman have for each other within the boundaries of a true faithful relationship was still a mystery to me. I had caught the briefest glimpse of it with Tris, but never had it before or since.

Looking back, I can actually thank Clinton for that day. His betrayal brought everything out in the open – everything I had suppressed, denied, tried to pretend I had resolved, all fell out and was burned away in the heat of my anger. That was all thanks to the uncaring behaviour of yet another in a series of self-centred, exploitative narcissists that had come and gone from my life. Something broke in me that day. It broke, not to be mended, but to be thrown away forever. That part of me that was weak and insecure, that needed a man to complete my life, that sought the comfort of love at any cost, shattered and was tipped into the recycle bin of my life's history. As I stood and gazed at the shattered windscreen of Clinton's ugly old car, I somehow felt that those tiny shards reflected the part of me that had finally given in to the blows and the pressure. Like that piece of glass, it was now beyond repair – and good riddance, I thought. Good riddance to Clinton, good riddance to my mother, to Steve, Darel, to all of them, to all of this. They will never again affect my life in a negative way.

EPILOGUE: THE VIEW FROM THE TOP

"And one day she discovered that she was fierce and strong, and full of fire, and that not even she could hold herself back because her passion burned brighter than her fears."
Mark Anthony

About two years have now passed since the day when that final betrayal burst into the open. As I've worked through that rage and pain, the event has faded into history along with everything that came before it. I can now say that I can look back on that day and the many other previous dark days, from a broader perspective and even with a sense of humour, laughing at my various learnings and experiences. Most of all, I'm grateful for my friends who have always been there to share good times and offer support during the bad times.

178

Nigel had once said that he would visit me no matter where in the world I lived. Well, he did indeed keep to his word and subsequently visited us for seventeen holidays in South Africa. Each holiday was always planned to perfection, with as much enthusiasm as the last, and always became the highlight of our year. Our love for South African wildlife afforded us the opportunity to visit game reserves at Hluhluwe, Nambiti and various private game farms in Kwa Zulu Natal. Each game drive was filled will incredible sightings of impala, giraffe, zebra, rhino, elephants, buffalo and lion to mention just a few. One of my most memorable trips was to a cheetah sanctuary, I was astonished to actually cuddle a fully grown cheetah, its loud purr vibrating against my nervous body as it ran its raspy tongue along my hand.

At the time of receiving the lifechanging email from Sandra, another holiday was only three weeks away. This one was to mark Nigel's fiftieth birthday, an event for which a true milestone celebration had been planned: a trip to Cape Town for Nigel, Claire, Ty and me. However, this holiday was not going to turn out as planned for obvious reasons. What should have been a non-stop joyous occasion began with Nigel arriving at the airport to find me a sobbing wreck. For days, the tears just poured uncontrollably, with the birthday boy graciously offering me his shoulder, as he always had.

So, what gift do you give to your best friend after twenty-five years of incredible friendship? I decided to make a photo book capturing all of our South African adventures: shark cage diving – now that was a serious poop-your-pants occasion if there ever was one; a side-car adventure around the Cape peninsula; sightings of lions; interactions with elephants – feeding these beautiful giants and touching their magnificent tusks; quadbike safaris and ziplining canopy tours. Not to forget our one non-South African adventure, a trip to Dubai with Ty, where we rode a camel. We have laughed – oh how we have laughed: tear-inducing, belly-aching laughter.

I deeply appreciate all my friendships. It's the friends that we meet along the way that help us appreciate the journey. Friendship is a special gift, generously given, happily accepted and deeply appreciated. True friendship isn't about being inseparable, it's about being able to be separated and not feel like anything has changed between you. As Nigel would often remind me, "always remember we are under the same moon, looking up at the same stars." My friends – Nigel, Rachel, Reeni, Joanne, Claire and others – have been ever present comforts in all I have come through. They have pushed me to take necessary action when I hesitated, they have always lent a helping hand and most importantly, they have always brought love, light and humour in the coldest, darkest, saddest moments.

*

For the first time in my life I can truly say that I am now abundantly happy. Mine is not some fairy tale happiness arising from having reached a life of complete perfection – of course there's no such thing. My happiness is that of a person who has faced terrible lows and wonderful highs and can now maintain a smile, knowing full well that there is more of both to come. It is the contentment and excitement of knowing that I am better prepared than I have ever been both to deal with the pains and fully appreciate the pleasures of my past, present and future. For years, I tried to look for things, people and situations that would make me happy. I now know that happiness is a choice we have to make within ourselves. It never came to me because it had to come from within me.

I have climbed the steps out of my own personal hell, towards my own personal heaven. If indeed it is possible to reach the top of that ladder in this life, then I'm close to that pinnacle. Looking back on how far I have climbed, I can see all the key events of my life in a totally different way to when I first experienced them. In particular, those terrible dark patches, those slippery or broken steps that I thought would knock me off the ladder for good, take on a very different appearance in the light from up here. The people I saw as perpetrators now appear as teachers who – however unwittingly – taught me to be the person I am today. I have looked back on my experiences so many times over the years but I see them now as never before. Previously, the adversity never seemed to have any purpose. Now I can see that it did, and the positive outcomes are ever clearer to me.

I have been in the thick of the good and the bad each and every day of my life, working my way through each conversation, thought, experience and emotion, and let's be honest, it has been messy at times. I have examined and re-examined so many things that I otherwise might have tried to ignore. In fact, I spent many years trying to block them from my memory. This focused and conscious confrontation of my past has enabled me to see deeper into every major event in my life.

I believe we all need to find ways to assess our lives and to devise our own methods and systems to discover meaning and healing. My own experience has shown me that the key to finding meaning, and getting the results I really want, is the seemingly negative process of focusing on the things that have harmed me. Looking at the things I don't want, the people and events that have interfered with my happiness, and then systematically processing them to find positive meaning from each and every negative experience. My process has consisted largely of acknowledging and identifying all those trigger points of potential negative emotions and thoughts, and then making a conscious effort to be positive no matter what. I have long believed that positivity is my superpower.

Whilst I will never forget the bad things that have happened to me, I am rapidly forgetting the pain they caused and the desires they ignited for vengeance, justice or vindication. Every time I think of the people who have wronged me in my life, I realise that the pain they have caused me has dissipated a little more since the last time they crossed my mind, and I am even more focused on building the life I have envisioned.

A mother's betrayal... that is what lies at the core of the deep, suppressed trauma that has haunted me for decades. You may expect that the most traumatic part of my childhood was the sexual abuse. Actually, that has not been the most difficult thing to process at all. My abuser was a sick man, a predator, and he found an opportunity and took it. Twisted as it is, there is a sad and sordid logic and consistency in his actions. However, what has been most difficult for me to deal with is my mother – the woman who was supposed to be my nurturer and protector, who was supposed to love me. The woman who ensured that my abuser never faced any consequences for his crimes. Why did she let it happen? Why did she never love me? Why did she never even acknowledge it?

In all my attempts to re-establish a relationship with her, and to try and make sure that Ty at least had a grandmother, no answers to these questions have ever arisen. They never will and I am now at peace with that. I can never begin to understand her, her motivations, her traumas and fears. I no longer need to know why she allowed Steve to do what he did, laying the foundation for years of trauma and dysfunction. I realised, years before I had even begun to process all of this, that the best thing I could do to make up for my lack of a good mother was just to become an amazing one myself. I managed to raise a strong, well-adjusted, self-reliant, confident and loving young man who is ready to go out into the world and pursue his own dreams and goals. Left to raise him entirely on my own, I am so proud of him, but also of the mother I have become.

We are a beautiful family, bonded forever.

Once I accepted that I would never erase my past, I began to make peace with it and as I did so, something completely unexpected happened. Through all the years I was dealing with the ghosts of my past over and over, my life's direction was dictated to a large extent by the men I fell in love with. That spell was finally broken after that climactic betrayal was revealed. After that, as I faced my past head-on and the ghosts gradually started to dissipate, I found myself falling in love again – with myself! It took me three decades to realise that self-love is the foundation of any happy life. Many wise people have pointed this out before, but I only truly understood it when it started to happen for me. This is not the fake self-regard that I saw in the four perpetrators of those betrayals; that's not self-love at all – that's an empty compensation for the lack of self-love. Perhaps that's the reason I attracted two narcissistic men: to reflect my own lack of self-love until I finally saw it.

Those were all devastatingly hard lessons, but ultimately I did learn from them. There were times when I thought they would break me, but somehow I managed to maintain a pure heart and a strong mind to overcome all of it. My spirit chose to stay positive and rise above it all. I don't believe that I'm unique in this. I am just one expression of the unbreakable human spirit. I hope, however, that my story can help other people experiencing similar adversity in their lives to find that spirit within themselves.

I have learned several core principles from my experiences,

especially the power of a positive mindset and self-belief to transcend all challenges. Our circumstances and the things that happen to us are never really within our control. What is always in our control are our emotions and the way we respond to people and events. Visualise clearly, and use your emotions as the guides they are meant to be. They are not there to control us; it is up to us to control them and to follow their prompting. Chase your dreams as if your life depends on them because the truth is, it absolutely does!

As I formulate these closing thoughts, I stand on Table Mountain after a long hike to the top, during a visit to Cape Town. This is the second time I have done this, though the situation is very different to the last occasion. Last time I climbed these slopes was on that fiftieth birthday trip I organised for Nigel when I was on the verge of falling apart. The climb then was a desperate slog out of despair, my mind doing somersaults at every step, today it's a victory hike. It may not be the world's highest mountain, but summiting any mountain feels like a conquest. It really does feel like standing on top of the world. Below me, on one side, the city of Cape Town sprawls out among the peaks with the vast, blue Atlantic beyond. On the other side, stretching towards the horizon, is the interior of the country I have called home for nearly two decades. From this height, in any direction, the truly endless nature of possibility is made clear. I stand at the centre of a vast circle of potentiality, stretching in all directions and its only limit is my own field of vision. I realise now that this infinite range of opportunity has always been there, but it required the arduous climb to this height to be able to see it. The series of twists and turns that has brought me from rural Wales to the southern tip of Africa, is really quite wondrous when I stop and think about it. Whether it's by chance or intent, it's incredible either way. How many of us are just trudging through our lives, never realising that each of us is a protagonist in an amazing story, the plot and events of which are as unique as our fingerprints?

Where to from here? I can't say yet. More unexpected turns are yet to come and I cannot wait to take them. From where I stand, it may appear that this is the end of a journey, but really it is only the beginning. It doesn't matter which direction I choose – the ocean of possibility to the west and north, or the undulating landscape of adventure to the east – the ensuing journey will likely surpass the path I have already taken. So I stand and watch and dream a while, and know that when the time comes to move, regardless of the direction taken, I will be moving ever forward, happy and at peace.

It doesn't matter what has been written in my story so far, it's now a question of how I fill up the rest of the pages. Looking ahead, turning the page, I embrace the next chapter as it unfolds before me.

W.R.

May 2019